0804

39p

Richar

CW00740442

Chronicles of a
Victorian Detective

P & D Riley (Publishers)

First Published 1907 as 'Lancashire's Crime and Criminals'
This Edition First Published 1995

Published by P & D Riley,
12 Bridgeway East,
Runcorn,
Cheshire,
England.

ISBN: 1 874 712 18 2

Typography and this edition copyright © by P & D Riley

British Library Cataloguing - in - Publication Data
A Catalogue Record for this book is available from the British Library.

Printed in England
Typeset in Times New Roman and Cooper Black
by Adam & Donna Riley

Contents

Richard Jervis pictured in retirement

Editor's Note

The rarety value of memoirs of Victorian Police Officers is acute, so it is with great pleasure that we present the reminiscences of Richard Jervis, who rose from the humble rank of constable to superintendent in the Victorian era, serving as he did throughout old Lancashire, then a much larger county than it is today. With the geographical size of the county at that time came enormous responsibility for those in position of power, made all the more remarkable bearing in mind the lack of communications enjoyed by today's police forces, and the lack of resources generally.

Mr Jervis's account of police work in his 57 years is also a demonstration of the dedication necessary at that time, a dedication it is hard to understand today. For that reason alone these notes are worth re-publishing almost ninety years after they first appeared. They are a social history and a local history combined, and will surely be welcomed by anyone with a fascination for the past despite their relatively localised nature.

History is history, and policework is policework and both provide a unique insight into how our forefathers worked and thought when presented in the form of memoirs. It is hoped therefore that the memoirs of Mr Jervis will be welcomed by historians and general readers alike. In order to make the book more readable, some passages of strong traditional Lancashire dialect have been deleted which will not please everyone but will, it is hoped, make the work easier to understand by those not familiar with the North of England.

Peter Riley
1995

Acknowledgements

The editor would like to thank the following for their invaluable help in the preparation of this book:

Tony Ashcroft of Leigh Library, Lancashire, for first bringing this book to our attention.

Adam Riley, for his perseverance in taking up the mantle of typesetting this book from the original, often badly flawed original edition.

Donna Riley for her help with layout and design.

INTRODUCTION

Mr Richard Jervis, the author of these "Reminiscences," claims Shropshire by birth, but it was in Lancashire that he passed his eventful life, and gained those experiences which gave to his notes more than a passing interest. Coming of a family who have held long and honourable positions in the Police Force of the country, it was only natural that he should turn to that avocation with the facility of the duck for water; and, having decided upon his career, provided with grit, perseverance, and a fine sense of duty and honour, it was only natural that he should succeed. Not succeed merely from a worldly point of view, in obtaining position, means, and influence, honourable though are where gained without dishonour, but succeed in that better sense of having made his world all the better for having lived therein. It is lamentable that too many men, regarding work as an irksome necessity, are firmly resolved to do as little labour as possible with the least expenditure of energy, while at the same time they are keenly sensitive on the subject of wages. Such men as these found by the thousand huddled together at the bottom of the hill, raging against those who pass them by towards the summit, eternally complaining of the ill-luck which refuses to give them a push up towards the heights crowned with the success and glory. These are the men whom are the last to come and the first to go when financial stress bids the employer economise; he who is perpetually referring to his "bond" to confirm him in his slothfulness is never destined to be anything more than a makeshift. And it is not the Fates, but his own freewill which so dooms him.

Mr Jervis began life with the determination to get away from the crowd, to make something of himself more than a mere number, to reach the highest point his profession permitted him. His methods to this end were simple, so simple that they are overlooked by the multitude in the race of life. He always kept himself educated in advance of his particular rank at the time, he put Duty first and last, and as its guardian angles he called Sobriety, Truth, Civility, and Perseverance. He never objected to working overtime, and he never pressed for the immediate payment of the same. As a young constable in the days when the Force was not the highly organised system of to-day, he saw laxity of discipline, unreliability of many members. When he rose to positions of authority, he enforced discipline and order with a vigour which made the do-littles and-less-if-we-can squirm, but which gladdened the hearts of communities suffering from inefficient police administration. He was a terror to the skulker, but in his long official career no dutiful man could ever say justly that he was not firm friend and helper.

Nor did Mr Jervis ever consider that the whole of his duty lay in the repression and detection of crime; he always insisted that the prevention of crime was as much the business of the police as its discovery and punishment; and in every district of Lancashire in which he was placed, he set to work to remedy social evils, whose offspring are lawlessness and criminality. He denounced over crowding, insanitary dwellings, and the excessive number of drinking dens. In this way he made many enemies among the class whose pockets where touched, and he was unceremoniously advised to "stick to his policing." But, undaunted, he held on his way, and now in his retirement he has the satisfaction of knowing that he was bequeathed good works to be enjoyed by the future generations. Would that the Police Force throughout the kingdom were animated by a like spirit! Its capabilities for social reform are vast, and if put into action would in a few decades entirely change the character of many of our towns and cities.

Mr Jervis joined the Lancashire County Constabulary as the youngest constable, and he was the youngest officer in all the successive ranks he gained. He obtained his inspectorship within seven years, being then twenty-five years of age, and less than seven years later he obtained the rank of superintendent, a position he held for 43 years, retiring in 1907 as the senior superintendent of England, and with the remarkable record of 57 years of service. In that period he has seen police duty in every part of Lancashire over which the County exercises jurisdiction; he has seen the growth of villages into populous towns, noted a marked improvement in the habits of the people, learned to love the Lancashire people for their grit, manliness, humour, and "jannockness."

Mr Jervis has been on duty-mounted or a-foot-attending on Royalty at nearly every Royal visit to Lancashire since 1850. He had the honour of speaking to her late Majesty, Queen Victoria; the old Duke of Wellington and Lord Palmerston-two names which seem to us of the present generation to belong to the remote history of England. On the visit of the Prince of Wales several years ago, to Lathom House, Lord Crichton introduced Mr Jervis to his Royal Highness, who, in a pleasant chat with the senior police officer of England, was facetious over his reputed dislike to the motor car. But the worthy superintendent assured the Prince that after his recent experience in an automobile he found it exhilarating.

Mr Jervis has lived to see the passing of old systems and the coming in of new. In his own particular line, he has witnessed vast changes in Police administration. Half a century ago, it was a matter of doing duty-with the logwood or truncheon. In these days the Police have to proceed almost on the Salvation Army style. They have to plead and coax, be civil in the midst of incivility, give the soft answer which turneth away wrath. The virtue of the constable's staff, once most potent in quelling rows, has decayed, and a policeman must be kind and gentle in the most aggravating circumstances.

For fifty years, Mr Jervis conducted all police and criminal prosecutions before the magistrates in different parts of the county where he had been posted, and in the most serious cases he prepared the briefs for the prosecuting counsel at the

Assizes and Quarter Sessions. He had a wonderful memory for "decided cases", a keen eye for the telling points in a case, and a fluency of speech which frequently disconcerted aspiring advocates. He was as thorough in the preparation of his cases as in the discharge of his ordinary duty, and his commendations by judges and chairmen of Quarter Sessions have been numerous. preparation of his cases as in the discharge of his ordinary duty, and his commendations by judges and chairmen of Quarter Sessions have been numerous.

Mr Jervis on his retirement was granted a pension of two thirds of his salary by the standing Joint Committee of Lancashire, and subsequently attending a meeting of the committee he personally received the encomiums of those with whom he had long been officially acquainted. Colonel Moorsom, Chief Constable of the County, spoke highly of his services; Mr. E.B. Dawson, barrister-at-law, chairman of the County Quarter Sessions, and the Lancashire bench, came down specially from Lancaster to bid the worthy superintendent "good-bye," and to bear his testimony to his character as a man and officer; while Mr. W.S. Barrett, Chairman of the County Council, and Deputy Chairman of the Liverpool County Quarter Sessions, wrote: "I am very sorry that I shall not be at the meeting of the Standing Joint Committee on Thursday, as I understand Superintendent Jervis will tender his resignation. I should like to have expressed my very great regret that he is leaving the Force and my very high appreciation of his long and faithful services. I have known him about 30 years, and know his worth. I believe he has made it part of his business to prevent crime as well as to detect it, and personally know of more than one case where his kindly advice has restored persons to the paths of rectitude. On my behalf please wish him health to enjoy his well-earned retirement."

The eulogy of the Ormskirk Bench and Court Officials and the Press was equally warm, and the mere enumeration of the tangible tokens of appreciation he has received would make a long list.

His retirement, after so long a service, has opened out a question, which it is to be hoped will not be shelved. It arose in this way: Mr Jervis's record was brought to the notice of the Home Office by Mr. H. Lindon Riley, barrister-at-law, and the reply from that department indicated that the absence of any Royal Order of Merit for the Police was receiving attention, which is likely to bear fruit. The letter from Mr Gladstone's assistant was in the following terms:-

Dear Sir,-

In reply to your letter of the 26th inst. about Superintendent Jervis, I am desired by Mr. Gladstone to thank you for your letter, and to say he regrets that he has no means of distinguishing a police officer for long service by recommending him for a decoration. The Imperial Service Order is not, as you are no doubt aware, applicable to the police. I am to add, however, that the fact that there is no corresponding decoration which can be awarded to the Police is at present under consideration.

The desirability of the institution of such an Order in regard to a service, the members of which have often to risk life and limb in behalf of the peace and order of a community must be obvious to anyone who knows that the dangers encountered by the Police Force are many and its rewards are few, and we hope that Mr. Riley's characteristic pertinacity will not fail him on this question until the "consideration" of the Home Office has passed into the establishment of an Order of merit for the Police Force. Why it should have been so long neglected in the face of the creation of Distinguished Service Orders in other branches of public life is one of those things "no feller can understand."

CHAPTER ONE

AFTER much hesitation and consideration I have been induced to give way to the solicitation of my friends. They assured me that fifty-seven years' service in the Lancashire Constabulary - which I only relinquished in August, 1907, and which then constituted me the oldest police officer in England - must abound with incidents interesting to the general police and instructive in many ways to various classes of the community. Now I have often looked with regret upon the passing of men whose lives, rich in activity and interest, might in their reminiscences have enriched local history and contributed most materially to the elucidation of the factors which have played their part in the rise and growth of communities. For while we have general histories of localities, it is the personal and individual, with its little touches of gossip and of neighbourliness, which possesses an everlasting charm for the ordinary man, and often enables him to understand the meaning of important events which sprang from petty and casual beginnings. Hence it is that, though I have no great desire for writing, I feel constrained to offer my reminiscences to the public in the hope that some of them may be found of interest, and that from them may be drawn lessons of instruction for the present generation.

No man liveth to himself, least of all a police officer, and trained to observation, discipline, and the weighing of evidence, for and against, his impressions of towns and peoples cannot be without value, if intelligence has its full play in the task.

I was born in Shropshire in 1832. My father became connected with the Police Officer of Lancashire in 1838, and his stations were at Liverpool, Rainhill, Southport, Old Swan, Bootle, Rochdale, and St. Helens. Very early in his service he was appointed Superintendent of the Rochdale Division, and later filled the same position in the St. Helens Division. I entered the Lancashire Constabulary on the 17th August, 1850. I was then the youngest member in the force, being eighteen years of age.

CHRONICLES OF A VICTORIAN DETECTIVE

It may perhaps be more acceptable to the general reader if for a short time I digress from the strictly personal to give a few of my recollections of Southport when I first knew it, viz, from 1842 to 1845.My father was then the first inspector for the town, and he had control of a "force" of one constable - No. 15, Edward Ashworth, whose beat comprised Southport and Birkdale! Church-town, Crossens and Banks, and Formby had also a constable each. There was then a charge of twopence for admission on to the Promenade. Poor old Caesar Lawson was the toll collector, and his hut at which he collected the coppers stood near to the site of the present Pier entrance. Visitors to the town were conveyed in Labray's coach - "The Swallow", I believe, was its name, and it met passengers in the afternoon at Scarisbrick Bridge, to which they were brought in canal boats from Manchester. The highway between Southport and Scarisbrick ran through Blowick, entering Manchester Road opposite to the old Rectory. Scarisbrick New Road was occupied by sandhills - the home only of the rabbits, and the yellowness of their sands relived only by starr grass. I saw the first sod cut in Hoghton Street. Before this was laid out the way to Holy Trinity Church lay through the sandhills. The Rev. Jonathan Jackson was for many years the respected pastor, and Mr James Molyneux (plumber) the clerk.

How can the modern resident conceive it? A brook noted for watercress ran along the Manchester Road side of the church!

I attended Mr Richard Wright's school in London Street, and it was almost surrounded by sandhills. One afternoon we had a couple of hours leave from lessons to listen to speeches by John Bright and Richard Cobden. They spoke from the balcony of the Victoria Hotel. Cobden was the one who made the greatest impression on us as lads. Speaking in favour of the reduction of taxation of various goods, he was particularly emphatic in regard to sugar - the cheapest of which was then 9d a pound! And he dwelt upon its nourishing qualities for children of all ages. "Our mothers," said Cobden, " put the sugar basin upon the topmost shelf of the cupboard, and warned us saying: ' Now, children, you must not touch that sugar because it will ruin your teeth!' Of course she knew better than that, but the high price was practically prohibitive to those of us with moderate means."

We return to school red hot politicians - Whig and Tory, for this was before the days of Radicals and Conservatives. In the course of our debates one lad argued convincingly for a reduction of the sugar tax. "Look here!" he said, "if sugar comes down to 4d. a pound. what a big lump of toffee we would get for a penny !" The was unanswerable! The boy was father to the man; he subsequently made a no inconsiderable name for himself in the commercial world.

I remember one night a strong westerly gale blowing, and I heard my father say to Ashworth that as it was not unlikely a wreck might be the result he was to visit the Birkdale shore about one o'clock in the morning. My application to accompany Ashworth was refused, but - "lads will be lads" - I went. When a little distance beyond the site upon which the Palace Hotel now stands we found sacks of flour strewn upon the shore; and a little further on three men were busily engaged in hauling one of the bags into the sandhills, but on our appearance they scampered off. That they had not been idle was proved by our discovery of four or five sacks lightly covered over with sand in the hills. It was then that enthusiasm for the Force filled me, and I said to Ashworth: "When I'm big enough I'll be a policeman."

The next tide brought up the bodies of four sailors from the ill-fated ship. They were buried at Holy Trinity Church, and the flour was conveyed to the Hoghton Arms yard.

I well remember the old Original Hotel and Mrs Allen's travelling theatrical booths, which used to be 'pitched' at the back of the hostelry.

In those days I knew everybody in Southport and Birkdale, but for the present we will leave the district to return to it as it appeared to me in 1857.

Having joined the Lancashire Constabulary, my first station was Bury. The uniform then included tail coats and tall heavy hats, lined in the crown and sides with leather. In addition to strong leather stocks, they carried staff, handcuffs, and heavy wooden rattles, while the night duty men in addition had lamps and logwood stocks. The police were called after Sir Robert Peel, who introduced the Police Bill, 'Peelers' and 'Bobbies', and the names have stuck well. In those days the police had rough times of it in Lancashire, their hours of duty heavy and long, their pay low. They had nine hours on - from 9pm to 6am, and no time was allowed off for supper, while in addition they had two hours duty in the day - from 3pm to 5pm. At the former hour the whole of the men were assembled to hear the routes read, and this reminds me of an incident which arose during my first weeks service. An old constable was showing me round a beat leading from Walmsley Road to Freetown, when about three o'clock in the morning we heard footsteps approaching from the direction of some waste land. We stood back in the shade; a man came up with a sack containing 'cops'; my companion questioned him; he gave his name and address in Freetown, and said that he had been at his brother's 'carding', and that he was taking the 'cops' from his house to his own to weave. His tale was believed, and he was allowed to go. At three o'clock pm parade that day the inspector read out the report: "Between the hours of six o'clock last night and five o'clock this morning, a cotton mill, belonging to Mr——, near Walmsley Road, was broken and entered and a quantity of 'cops' stolen."

My comrade of the early hours of that morning put up a warning finger to prevent me giving our experience, his plea being that as he was an old constable he would be dismissed. We went in search of the man, but of course he was 'not known'; and at my suggestion my crestfallen companion informed the inspector in the hope that some of the men might know the man from our description of him.

This occurrence was an excellent lesson to me, and only a week or so afterwards I met a young man on the Bolton Road. He carried a small parcel under his arm, containing an overcoat, which he explained belonged to his brother at Rochdale, and he was fraternally returning it to him. But I had a recent experience fresh in my mind, and I detained him. My doubts and fears were at rest when it was discovered that the man had broken into a house at Bolton and stolen the coat. This was my first case, and it made me a bit keen. I made almost a special feature of stopping and searching tramps and suspicious looking characters on the road, and the results justified the means - a great many did I pick up with stolen property in their possession.

I always found when respectable men were stopped during the night time and questioned, if questioned in a civil and proper manner, never or scarcely ever resented it. The manner is the thing especially with a policeman, either making or marring him.

CHRONICLES OF A VICTORIAN DETECTIVE

My first detective duty was in 1851, on the occasion of the 14th Earl of Derby - the Rupert of Debate - laying the foundation stone of the Athenaeum at Bury.

My first attendance on Royalty was in 1851. I was drafted along with others to Lancaster, the late Queen, Prince Albert, the Prince of Wales, and Princess Royal breaking their journey there from Balmoral to inspect the Castle. This duty extended to five or six days. From Lancaster the Royal party travelled to Croxteth and Worsley, where they remained two or three days, and which they reached by the Bridgewater Canal. I believe that it rained during every day of the visit. The police had no opportunity of drying their clothes, and their only sleeping accommodation was upon straw in schoolrooms. While at Worsley the Royal party drove upon one or two occasions to Manchester, and the 'Iron Duke' (the Duke of Wellington) was in attendance upon her Majesty. We had to regulate the traffic, and at one time there was a brief block upon the road. My post was opposite to the carriage of the Duke, and he asked me the cause of the delay.

Early one morning I had a curious experience in Bolton Street, Bury. I saw a white figure approaching as though it were that of an orthodox ghost. I stepped to the edge of the footpath, and by-and-bye, to my astonishment, I saw that it was a young lady wearing only her nightdress. She was fast asleep. I did not awaken her. Taking her by the arm I led her gently to the police office, where she was placed in a chair in front of the fire. She came to herself at length, and then it transpired that she was in the dangerous habit of walking in her sleep. One can imagine her consternation at finding herself in such surroundings in such peculiar circumstances.

CHAPTER TWO

THE SUAVE AND THE BELLICOSE ADVOCATE - A PRETTY NIGHT PLOT-
CIRCUMSTANTIAL EVIDENCE- MY FIRST MURDER CASE-
A MILITIA GARROTTER

I have often been struck by the contrast in police court advocacy and by its dismal failure in its purpose through the neglect of *suaviter in modo* while being too much intent upon *fortiter in re*. Let me give an instance. At one of my first courts a batch of about a dozen young people of both sexes were brought up charged with obstructing and annoying 'knobsticks' brought in during a strike or lock-out at one of the cotton mills. The defendants obtained the services of a Manchester solicitor, who had gained a great name in cases of that kind. He began his address to the magistrates in characteristic fashion, that is, by abusing them; declaimed that his clients could not expect to get justice from such a Bench, every member of which was interested in the cotton trade or allied industries; and so he went on in a similar strain greatly, no doubt to the joy of the 'gallery'. What was the result? Directly the fiery advocate had concluded his speech the chairman, without a word of comment, passed sentence - six weeks imprisonment.

Now for the contrast. The very next week another batch of people was brought up for a similar offence. They were defended by another Manchester solicitor, who, however, went upon quite different lines. His appeal was not as to lawless and unjust judges, but to considerate and sympathetic men of the world. He described his clients as poor uneducated persons who had been led into wrong by people old enough to be their fathers; unwittingly they had become law-breakers; he had pointed out to them the error of their ways, and they now desired him to say bow sorry and ashamed they were to appear before their Worships. "A soft answer turneth away wrath". The decision of the court was: "Discharged upon a promise not to repeat the offence."

The last time I met the first named advocate was forty years ago at the

16

the Rawtenstall Sessions, in my division. He appeared for my defence in a certain case, and the magistrates clerk, remembering his forensic fire of old, rather expected a little scene. But he and others who had known him in the past were agreeably surprised. He addressed himself in most gentlemanly and courteous terms to the Bench, and at the conclusion of the court I congratulated him upon his altered mode of advocacy. He smilingly admitted the soft impeachment; he had changed his style some time ago. "Ha!" commented the magistrates clerk. "Now tell me did your old style ever pay?" The other leaned forward, and in a confidential whisper replied: "No, but some people - who engaged me - thought it did."

After about eighteen months in Bury I was posted to the Blackburn Higher Division, and was stationed for a short time in Colne. Let me mention one case I had as illustrative of the difference between sentences then and now. A youth sixteen years of age for assaulting a girl of about the same age was sentenced to twenty-five years "transportation beyond the seas!" This was the form of sentence, and it was before the days of penal servitude.

It was here, too, that I was concerned in a case, which ultimately led to the abolition of a peculiar form of cruelty. Two men were in the habit of attending fairs with a nut barrow, which may be best described as a long stall on wheels, and which was drawn by two dogs. Early one Sunday morning they were returning from Burnley Fair over a newly-repaired road, sharp with new grit. These inhuman brutes were not content to be drawn upon the barrow by the dogs, but they were cruelly whipping them to increase their speed. The poor animals were limping with bleeding paws, and as one might very well imagine were in a distressed condition from the weight they had to drag. The men were summoned and severely punished. The Bench considered it a very cruel case; the Press took up the matter; they were supported by the member for the division, Colonel Wilson Patten, afterwards Lord Winmarleigh, and he was the means of securing an Act which made it an offence to put dogs to that kind of labour.

Circumstances arose out of the prosecution which showed me how villainy may manufacture false charges against an innocent person, and how, where mere "weight" of evidence is alone allowed to count, gross injustice may be done. In revenge for the active part I had taken against the two hawkers referred to, a couple of their pals had concocted a nice little plot against my character and liberty; but the workings of Providence are beyond the weak sight of poor mortals. A young woman who occupied a cellar beneath the room in which this plan was laid overheard all the details, and put me in possession of them at nine o'clock - just as I was going on duty - on the night when my disgrace had been resolved upon. The conspirators had impressed a girl - a niece - into their service. They had ascertained that I should return from a meeting point at Nelson, and arrive at one o' clock in the morning near a footpath on the Colne and Burnley Road. Upon my appearance the girl, who was to be a few yards in advance of the men, was to scream; then they would at once come to her assistance, and a serious offence was to be preferred against me. But it was another case illustrating that "the best laid plans o' mice and men aft gang agley". Shortly after I had entered upon duty I happened to meet a friend of the bold conspirators, and he made some remark about the weather. I put on a grim and determined look, and shook my logwood stick. I spoke emphatically: "There will be some rather rough weather about one o' clock in the morning, and if there is any virtue in this logwood there will be a case of manslaughter about that time!" He went away, wearing a worried look, and at the meeting point I told the constables that I felt sure I had spoiled the game. They insisted upon going back with me, but the plot was "off"; a messenger sent by the plotters' friend I had met duly warned them of the "excursions and alarums" in store for them.

This incident was not without a serious lesson to me; it taught me, indeed it satisfied me, and the truth of it I have often proved, that circumstantial evidence is much more reliable than what is called direct evidence, always provided, of course, that the circumstances are complete and that the chain is not broken. A number of circumstances, small in themselves, yet linked together, cannot lie. There is a dumb evidence more eloquent and convincing in truth than the words of a dozen human witnesses. These may lie, and do. Take the incident I have just mentioned. Had the plot not failed, and had I entered upon it unsuspectingly, there would have been my word, and against it the word of three witnesses!

In my short service of less than a year at Colne, a favourite pastime was the bowling of stones along the highway, the marks counting as they struck one another's bowls. Many a contest took place for wagers, and as in the excitement of the game little heed was taken of the traffic, pedestrians as well as horses were frequently injured - several seriously. I was rather sharp on these cases, and had brought a big gang of offenders before the magistrates, who always inflicted the full penalty - 40s. and costs. Some of them had determined to get even with me, and from information I received one Saturday night after the closing of the beerhouses I learned that a gang of them from fifteen to twenty young fellows armed with stones were waiting for me beneath a wall on the Windy Bank Road at Colne. My attention was to be attracted by the shrill scream of "Police!" as from a woman in trouble, and on my appearance the fusilade was to begin. In due course the soul-moving cry was raised, but instead of going down the road I went through the churchyard, and arrived at a spot where the ground was six or seven feet above the level of the road. There my 'friends' were congregated, and they spoke most ferociously against poor me. I dropped down in the midst of them. My logwood rattled against the wall. The valiant band scampered off, yet not before five or six of them got mixed up with my logwood, and to my surprise I afterwards learned that one of the men when he got home found that his arm was broken! There seemed to be an idea that I was the cause of it, and a County Court action was threatened, but it ended in threats.

In those days, the stocks were in full swing at Colne. The penalty for drunkenness was 5s, or six hours in the stocks; for playing at 'pitch and toss' the fine was 3s 9d, or three hours in the stocks. The latter were wheeled into the middle of the town on the market day, either for the reason that the delinquents might have the pleasure of a greater number of admirers, or because they might be to the crowd a practical illustration that the way of transgressors is hard. But, alas! familiarity, if it does not breed contempt, often breeds indifference, and the stocks and their occupants seldom received more than a passing glance.

My next station was Burnley, where I was chiefly engaged in detective work, and being shortly promoted to the position of sergeant I returned to Bury. I had made a speciality of enlarging my acquaintance with travelling, as well as local, thieves and their haunts, and the knowledge frequently stood me in good stead. For instance: Early one morning going through a lodging house - I often did this to the great disgust of the lodging house keepers - I found a man, whom I knew to be a travelling thief, in bed. Between his bed and the mattress I unearthed a bundle of six silk handkerchiefs. I took him into custody, but on the way to the station, in a long narrow passage leading to the street, he struggled and kicked me severely on the legs. There I had not room to use my logwood, but directly we reached the open I felled him to the ground. There he lay for two or three minutes, and when we resumed our journey he was quiet enough -there was no kick in him. On reaching the station I found blood oozing from the lace holes of my boots, and my legs still bear the marks of that man's clogs; while there is a dividing line in the nail of my left hand middle finger, half of which was torn off in the struggle. But that man, if still alive, will be able to show on the right hand side of his head the mark of my logwood. It was ascertained that the handkerchiefs had been stolen from a draper's shop in Burnley, which had been broken into. Prisoner was committed for trial at the Preston Sessions, and he was sentenced to seven years transportation. But even here the prisoner did not take things quietly. While the jury were considering their verdict he had surreptitiously got one of his clogs off, and he threw it with great force at the Chairman as he was announcing his sentence. The aim was rather low, and the clog struck the wooden panelling at the exact spot where the head of the Clerk of the Peace, Colonel Wilson, had been a second before. He had just moved to speak to someone, and that fact he used to say saved his life. He was the father of the present prosecuting solicitor under the Food and Drugs Act for the County Council.

Not satisfied with this dastardly piece of work, the prisoner made a determined attempt to escape from the dock. He upset several of the turnkeys, and was eventually only overpowered by the assistance of one or two jurymen, whose box was close to the dock, and who scrambled over to help the warders.

About this time a murder was committed at Rochdale. A man and woman, apparently of the tramping hawker's class, had engaged a bed at a small public house, and the next morning she was found in bed with her throat cut. There was a knife in her hand to suggest suicide; but the man had disappeared. With a view of trying to gain some clue I was sent over to Rochdale, where my father was superintendent, but I failed to identify the body. In the superintendent's gig the inspector and myself scoured the different roads leading into the town. From a toll bar keeper we got a slight clue: He had seen a man and woman - (answering somewhat to the description of this couple) - going from the direction of Manchester to Rochdale on the night that the two took lodgings at the latter place. The time fitted in, the clue was followed up, and the man was in the course of a few days arrested near Todmorden, convicted and hanged. This was my first inquiry in a murder case; and I learned something. The sergeant first called in, on the discovery of the murder, was guilty of a serous error. He promptly took the knife from the dead woman's fingers. That should have been left for a medical man, whose training better fitted him to judge whether the knife was in the hand before, or had been put in after death, or whether by other signs it had been used as the weapon of self destruction. As it was when the doctor arrived he replaced the knife, and his evidence was that in that position it could not have been used by a suicide. I mention this incident merely to show how necessary it is for the police to be at all times on their guard. The sergeant's action in this case afforded the defending counsel, Mr Sergeant Wheeler, a good argument upon which to address the jury.

My knowledge of travelling thieves served me on another occasion in Bury. An old gentleman was garrotted one night upon an open piece of land behind the old Market Hall, and robbed of his watch and purse. On going through the lodging-houses I saw a woman whom I knew to be the companion of a travelling thief known as 'Jacques'. Although she stoutly maintained that she had not seen him for five or six weeks, I learned that she had arrived in the town early that night in company with a man who answered the description of Jacques. He was not found there, but he was known to be in the Preston Militia, due to assemble in that town in two or three weeks time. On the assembly of the regiment I went to Preston, ascertained Jacques' billet, and went to visit him about midnight. But in a back street near at hand a jollification was going on in one of the houses. I entered, and found it pretty well filled with Militiamen and others. Jacques was in the thick of the fun, and seeing me he called out jovially: "Hello, sergeant, how are yer?" and he came forward to shake hands. I promptly put the snaps on them, and took him to the police station. There, a gentleman was describing an attack which had been made upon him by a Militiaman very shortly before then; he had garrotted him, robbed him, and with his bayonet stabbed and killed his dog. I took hold of Jacques' bayonet and found fresh blood upon it. The gentleman looked at my prisoner and exclaimed: "I believe this is the man!" He was, for the stolen articles were found upon him, that case was not called. He was clearly connected with the Bury case, and for that he was sentenced to fifteen years transportation.

CHAPTER THREE

After serving in Bury for about a year on this occasion I left for Burnley, on the application of the superintendent, to act principally as detective-sergeant. Watching and searching the outbuildings round Pendle Hill-(immortalised by Harrison Ainsworth as the home of the Lancashire witches)-was an exciting piece of police work which went on for many weeks. Two notorious characters named Briggs and Dickinson were "wanted" for, among other offences, shooting with intent to murder the licensee of the Deerply Inn, situated between Burnley and Bacup. They had broken in to the inn when the licensee heard them, and on going downstairs they shot him, though happily not fatally, but the bullet lodged in his breast and could not be extracted. He was a man getting on in years, and was accustomed to attend the Burnley Market, at which, as well as at home, he was accustomed to repeat the story of his adventures with great gusto, and even to show with considerable pride the scar of the bullet. The rascals themselves, however, had fled to America, but after an absence of between one and two years they had returned about the time I went to Burnley, and they had been seen in the neighbourhood of Pendle Hill. Farmers and residents generally were greatly alarmed, and a strict watch was set round the Hill. One night a young constable set to watch on the Clitheroe side of the Hill was suddenly startled, about midnight, by two men bursting from the hedge side and rushing towards him. Acting upon the saying he who hesitates is lost, the policeman did not hesitate a moment; he promptly took to his heels and sped to a public-house not far away, where he told his moving story. Among the eagerly attentive company was a farmer, who ejaculated; "Briggs and Dickinson, they are! It's not thee lad they want, it's me!" It was the night of the Clitheroe Fair, and the farmer had a considerable sum of money in his possession. The company numbering five of six men, turned out armed with pitchforks, pokers and anything which was handy and weighty enough. But the rascals anticipating the alarm had again made good their escape, and once more they reached America. A short time afterwards there came a report that one of them was taken for some offence in that country and executed.

As for the poor constable who figured in this incident, he was so terribly 'chaffed' by his comrades that he resigned.

Let me refer to one burglary case at Burnley because of the curious light it seemed to throw upon a strange peculiarity in dogs. A jewellers's shop kept, I believe, by Mr Widdup, had been entered and about £200 worth of jewellery carried away. Now in the kitchenm the first room entered by the burglar, was a savage bull dog, which of all the species is generally supposed to be the most awkward handful a hostile person can have to deal with. Yet that dog gave no sign, and the jeweller himself expressed his conviction that the dog had been drugged. The question stood at that for the time. As I have said before, I had made a speciality of acquainting myself with both local and travelling thieves, their habits and haunts, and I at once missed a ticket-of-leave man and his companion. Suspecting that Rochdale and Manchester would be their direction, I took the first train to the former place, where my father was superintendent, and whose help I intended to solicit in placing men on the different roads. But as I passed Todmorden and just before the train entered a long tunnel to Littleborough, I saw the man I suspected and his companion walking along the road towards Rochdale. I left the train at Littleborough, and walked back towards Todmorden to a roadside public-house, where I quite expected they would call, and in this expectation I concealed myself behind the front door. In the course of a few minutes they entered and were walking into the parlour, or rather the 'snug', when I jumped out and pushed the man against the woman. She fell and the man sprawled over her. Her apron became loose, and jewellery was scattered over the floor. The man got up, astonished and beaten. "Well!" he swore, "this is th' cleanest cop I ever knew!" He was sentenced to 14 years transportation and the woman to seven years.

Now as to the dog. The general opinion of those who knew his disposition was that he had been drugged. I put the question to the prisoner in conversation. No, he had never drugged a dog in his life. There was no need. "However savage a dog may be," he said, "if you come upon him in a small room from which there is no escape he will lie low. In this respect dogs are cowards. If doors are open so they can pass from one room to another, then the case is different; they will fight."

CHRONICLES OF A VICTORIAN DETECTIVE

In towns where there are organised gangs of thieves certain breaches of crime are followed exclusively by certain criminals. Some stick to burglary and housebreaking, others to highway robbery, the 'talents' of others again are devoted to pocket-picking, while some cannot soar to anything greater than the robbing of hen roosts. And the singular point in the business, of much assistance to the observant detective, is that they each, as a rule, stick to their own peculiar line.

I once had a man for stealing a wheelbarrow. It was proved that in his career he had stolen forty-eight wheelbarrows! I had another for the theft of a potato fork. He had stolennupwards of fifty of them! This fascination for particular kinds of booty is worth studying . When a robbery of a certain kind was committed I knew pretty well in what direction to look. For instance: a farm bailiff for a genmtleman near Blackburn was returning from Great Harwood Fair, when he was attacked by four men and robbed. Only a very meagre description of the men could be given, but we had four men who were capable of just this kind of offence. I arrested them, and after two or three remands evidence was obtained against them sufficient for their committal to the Liverpool Assizes, and there the chain of circumstantial evidence proved so complete against them that they were convicted by the jury and sentenced to seven years each.

"Playing possum" is a game which at times is worth cultivating by the detective who is more anxious for certain 'scoring' than more showy but less doubtful play. There had been a number of better-class residences and grenhouses stripped of lead. One night a gentleman came to me and informed me that he had just seen two men looking round his premises. I went with him, and we came suddenly upon the two "suspects". They were startled, and were for off, but I at once began to talk of the Liverpool races, for their special edification, and my "sporting" phraseology seemed to reassure them. They were not men suspected of thieving, but I felt that the birds were limed, and I told the gentleman I would have them before the week was out. The second night afterwards they were caught; I met them coming from Padiham way with a sack well-filled with lead; and they were each sentenced to eighteen months.

Let me quote another Burnley case to illustrate the extreme severity of sentences in those days. At an early hour one morning I heard a cry of "Police!" in the direction of a street, called "Wapping," then of bad repute. On making my way thither I met a woman who was followed by an old man. Close to the spot where I stopped her she dropped either a purse or watch - I forget which. Taking her to the station, and passing a man standing in a doorway, the old man said: "That man is as bad as the woman; he threatened me that if I followed her and did not 'shut up' he would break my —— head." I locked him up also. He had been working up to six o'clock the previous night, and it was only during the previous two or three weeks that he had been led astray by bad company. But he was sentenced to fourteen years transportation and the woman to seven! It was just at the time of the outbreak of a number of garrotte outrages, which, while terrorising people throughout the country, had aroused a determination among judges and chairmen of Quarter Sessions to use strong measures to stamp out the evil. And anything which bore the slightest resemblance to that offence was regarded with a severe ey. Now had this case occured today, it would probably have been a mere matter of the parties entering into sureties to be of good behaviour.

I have always insisted upon the necessity of cultivating the faculty of keen and intelligent observation if the policeman would be successful in his calling. Let me give an instance from my own notebook. Fifty three years ago there were on the outskirts of Burnley, on the Colne road, a number of small gardens cultivated by artisans. Walking through them one Sunday afternoon I noticed a shed, the timber of which had the appearance of railway sleepers or 'props'. At a short distance away the L. and Y. Railway ran over a small brook, the bridge over which was supported similar to those which went to the make-up of the shed. I sent for the railway officials, and the engineer came down. On viewing the bridge he was instantly alarmed. Timber had been drawn from its support, and hurrying workmen up to the spot he declared that not a minute was to be lost in making the bridge secure again, for the first heavy train passing over would cause it to collapse and thus lead to a frightful disaster. I arrested the man who had sold the props to the artisan, and he admitted that he had stolen them from under the bridge. The chairman of the Quarter Sessions, in sentencing him to seven years' penal servitude, described his offence as a heinous one. For the sake of a few shillings he had been perfectly callous as to the mischief and loss of life which his thievingmight have caused, and which would undoubtedly have happened had it not been for the prompt action of the police.

CHRONICLES OF A VICTORIAN DETECTIVE

My first attendance on Royalty was in 1851. My next in 1855 or 1856, on the occasion of the Queen's visit to Manchester. While I was in charge of a body of men at Pendleton, the Mayor came down in a cab enquiring for me. He had her late Majesty Queen Victoria's Despatch Box in his possession, to be delivered intothe hands of Lord Palmerston. he had an important engagement to attend to, and he asked me to deliver the box personally. Taking his cab I discharged the duty. I found his lordship very agreeable, and polite, inquisitive as to the police arrangements which had been made for her Majesty's visit. I was puzzled to know why I had been selected for this duty by the Mayor until a short time afterwards Mr. Heelis, a Manchester man and chairman of our Bench, smilingly asked me if I had had a pleasant chat with Lord Palmerston. I then knew how the Mayor had found my humble self.

About this period I heard a characteristic story told of Lord Palmerston. His Lordship was travelling North and had alighted at a wayside station. The carriage of the gentlemen whom he was visiting not having arrived, he was enjoying a smoke as he walked down the platform. The station-master bustled up to him, swelling with authority and outraged dignity, and brusquely informed him that smoking was not allowed on the platform - a regulation which was common in thos days. Lord Palmerston bowed to authority and threw away his cigar. By-and-bye the carriage arrived for his Lordship, and the horrified station-master, learning who the gentleman was, went to his Lordship, and, in a most obsequious manner, began to apolgise. But he was contemptuously waved aside, his Lordship cutting him short with the words: "I thought you were an Englishman doing your duty; now, I consider you a cur."

In 1857 I was appointed Inspector of Southport and district. I will pass over the generous tributes paid to my services by the magistracy and Press of East Lancashire, but with genuine pleasure do I place on record my testimony to the good traits in the character of the East Lancashire folks. Truly, they are 'gradeley' folks - the most hospitable and generous I have ever met. Innumerable are the scenes of practical sympathy I have witnessed among the very poor. Poor in this world's goods, old people of what they had. In bitterly cold weather, late at night, early in the morning, I have known them carrying hot gruel and what they could make to cheer and comfort poor bedridden creatures, sometimes stricken with fevers, who often times lived some distance away. Poverty is a hard lot, and it would become a hopeless despair were it not for the kindness of the poor to the poor.

Upon the rise and fall of people in East Lancashire I could write a book. I knew several to be millionaires, and others who approached that position. They started with nothing; even their little education was gained at the night school; but they had industry and perseverance, and not content with a day's work they kept busy at their looms half through the night - their only light a halfpenny candle.

Edwin Waugh, whom I once met at a friend's house in Rochdale forty-five years ago, admirably portrays the people of that district, and has drawn characters I have recognised over and over again.

As an example of the other side of the picture, the gentleman at whose house I met Edwin Waugh was then worth £30,000. He died practically a pauper - extravagant living had ruined him; and two of his children are now leading vagrant lives.

CHAPTER FOUR

WOMEN THIEVES AT SOUTHPORT - THE BURIED CASHBOX
A CHASE ON HORSEBACK - 'HIS DARLING POLLY'

In 1857 I was appointed Inspector of Southport and district. The place was then a seaside village, small, yet not without an attractive prettiness of its own. Since then what changes have taken place! I question whether there are more than half a dozen persons now living in Southport who were resident therein when I first knew it 65 years ago. At my appointment in 1857 the police force, I believe, numbered ten for Southport, Crossens, Banks, Birkdale, Ainsdale and Formby. The same ground must now be covered by a force of about a hundred.

Fortunately Southport has never been a place for serious crime; the principle deviation from the strict paths of integrity consisted in little petty thefts - very annoying, of course, unless we caught the thieves.

The two best known characters were each named 'Charles Hesketh'. One was notorious; he lived at Marshside, and was a frequent visitor at the Police Court. The other was the beloved Rector - a grand old English gentleman. One day I met the latter in Lord Street, and smilingly pointing to a newspaper placard upon which was inscribed in large type, "The Notorious Charles Hesketh Again," he said: "I see you are determined to keep up my notoriety."

During my inspectorship, Barnum, the great showman, with 'General Tom Thumb' as one of his great attractions, visited Southport from Manchester, and the show was followed by some very clever pickpockets, with the result that there was scarcely a performance at which ladies were not robbed. On one occasion two young ladies from Denton, near Manchester, came into my office, then on the first floor of the Town Hall, and complained that a purse belonging to one of them had been stolen, containing, among other property, the half of a second class return ticket from Manchester. The ladies, sisters, had that morning booked second class return from the city to Southport. I asked the sister who had escaped the attention of the 'light fingered gentry' to allow me to see her ticket, and I took the number of it. Hurrying to the railway station, Mr Williams, the station master, a most obliging official, was good enough to send a telegram for me to Pendleton, the collecting station for Manchester, requesting that if anyone presented a ticket with a number following the one I had taken he should be detained. Within half an hour or so there came a reply: "Ticket has been presented and person is detained here." I went over by the next train and found the man in custody. He was said to be one of the smartest thieves in Manchester; the case was clearly brought home to him, previous convictions were proved, and he was sentenced to fourteen years penal servitude.

Barnum, before the finish of the performance, was informed of the capture, and was so delighted that he announced the fact to the audience. He was a man with a splendid knowledge of men and thing, and with abilities which would have helped to make a name in other walks than that of the showman. Once I ventured to suggest to him that he would have made a capital policeman, and he laughed: "Why, yes; I've often had a thought that detective work would just about suit me."

Upon another occasion pickpockets were at work at a bazaar held in the Town Hall, and it was reported that two young ladies, visitors at the Rectory, had lost their purses. I had just noticed two women going in the direction of the railway station. They were well dressed enough, and were got up as ladies calculated to deceive the unwary; but there was an artificiality, a sham, about them which impressed me, and accepting all risks I followed them, and requested them to follow me to the police station. There I left them in charge of a constable while I went to the bazaar, and after a brief interview with the young ladies I brought them to the office to see if they had noticed the two women near them. That was unnecessary, under the chairs on which the women sat were two purses! They were at once identified by the ladies as their property, the women admitted their guilt, and proving to be old offenders they were eventually sent into penal servitude.

CHRONICLES OF A VICTORIAN DETECTIVE

In 1859 or 1860 I had a post office case in Southport. There were frequent complaints of letters containing money, etc, having been stolen, and the local office, which was then in Lord Street, was suspected. An official from the General Post Office - a very intelligent young man - came to see me, and we arranged that test letters should be posted, he undertaking that duty. The third morning after this plan had been adopted, he informed me that one test letter had not been received, and together we went to the post office, where the chief clerk and other officials were assembled. I gave them a description of the missing letter, bluntly told them that it had been stolen, that I was going to search for it, and that I should begin at the head of the department. The chief clerk seemed agitated and flurried. He emptied his pockets reluctantly, and finally there came forth marked stamps and coins, which had been placed in the missing envelope. He admitted his guilt, and he was sentenced to five years penal servitude.

Perjury, often too common even today in our Law Courts, on one occasion so unblushingly reared its head in the Southport Police Court that I prosecuted the man for the offence at the Assizes. It was said to have been the first of its kind from the district, there was a conviction with a sentence of eighteen months imprisonment, the judge complimented the police upon having taken up the case, and its result was to purify - for a time at least - the atmosphere of the local Police Court.

During my five year service at the seaside the Commissioners had bestirred themselves in improving the town. A pier had been erected, while as for the Promenade whose lengths of it had to be rebuilt several times, so difficult was it in those days to cope with the encroaching tides. Then there was little room for sarcasm at the coyness of the sea. It was no uncommon thing to see the tide in Lord Street as far as the Scarisbrick Arms Hotel.

I carried away with me a substantial token of the residents' appreciation of my services in the form of a gold watch bearing this inscription: "presented to Mr. Richard Jervis, Inspector of Police,

CHRONICLES OF A VICTORIAN DETECTIVE

December, 1862, by a few friends, as a token of esteem for his valuable public services in Southport"; and for about eighteen months subsequently I was stationed at Ormskirk. It was a sleepy old town in those days, with the exception of Saturday and Sunday nights, when fights were frequent and sometimes furious. John Barleycorn, of course, being the ringleader in most of the affrays. A wonderful change has taken place in that respect during the last forty-six years. Then, one heard better class tradesmen over their morning 'liveners' exclaim ruefully, though not without a touch of pride; "Eh, I was jolly well drunk last night; I don't remember going home; I rather fancy a policeman looked after me." Now, if the same class of people get drunk they are certainly not the first to publish their over-indulgence to the world. Shame now exists where once there was open pride, showing that drunkenness is robbed of the respectability in which it was once clothed by the middle-class. Eighty per cent of the manifest drunkenness is in these days confined to the lowest class - the slum dweller, the casual labourer, the loafer, and many who are of criminal habits. This I take to be a good sign of the times, and I venture the prediction that if the improvement is maintained with equal steps during the next forty years we shall see a sober England, without even the aid of new Licencing Acts. Increased education and the enlargement of facilities for cheap and rational recreation and amusement have tended greatly to the improvement of the character and conduct of the working classes, breeding in them a distaste for intemperate drinking.

Keeping an eye upon strangers in those days was sometimes useful to policemen. Let me give an instance from my own notebook. We had received a "route" from Preston respecting a shop there which had been broken into, and a cash box containing a considerable sum of money had been stolen. No descriotion of the thief could be given, but it was hazarded that he had gone in the direction of Liverpool. I sent men to watch the Liverpool road. I happened to see a smart looking man, a stranger, enter a hairdresser's shop in Aughton Street, kept my Mr Lea. I followed, and found him in the act of having his hair cut. I questioned him as to whence he came and whither he was bound. He was highly indignant ; talked about the "liberty of the subject," and was full of bounce generally, but he could give no satisfactory account of himself, and I escorted him to the police station. He was in possession of a considerable sum of money, among which was a peculiar coin described in the "route". That did for him. He admitted the offence, Nay, he did more. He took me to a field just outside Preston, where he had hidden the cash box. He was committed for trial at the Preston Sessions, and received a long term of imprisonment. In that case the prosecuting solicitor handed the brief to a young barrister - his first case. His son became a rather prominent member of the Bar, and his grandson now pleads in the Northern Circuit.

The owner of the cash box sent me a handsome silver knotted stick, upon which was a flattering inscription respecting the catcher.

For several weeks we were annoyed by robberies from boatmen's houses on the canal bank between Liverpool and Burscough. Once or twice a week cottages were entered, and the remarkable thing in nearly every instance was not only that there seemed a gin bottle in the cupboard of each house, but that the thieves always helped themselves to it as well as any money and clothing they could find. Maghull and Lydiate had suffered considerably from the scamps, and I mentioned to a doctor friend of mine their peculiarity as to the drink. He offered to mix a bottle which, although harmless in a way, would clip the wings of the night hawks for a time. I gave the "medicine" to the sergeant at Burscough, and he arranged with the occupier of a house likely to be entered for its disposal. But a dose was not required. The thieves were taken that very night at a cottage not far from the one where the "soothing syrup" awaited them; a number of cases were proved against them, and they were sent to penal servitude.

One of my most exciting hunts was at Ormskirk. Late one afternoon in the autumn of 1863 I was in Lathom, near "Charlesbye", when I met a military officer galloping in the direction of Lathom House. He was a member of one of the oldest county families, and I will refer to him as the "Captain". He seemed madly excited, and as he flew along he waved his sword and yelled "Fenians!" A little further on I came across an

Irishman, at whom the Captain had fired a pistol and blown away a portion of his coat collar. Near Mr Roper's, "The Cranes", Crane's Lane, I met the Captain returning towards Ormskirk, in the company of the late Sergeant Major Nunnerley. I held up my hand, and called upon the Captain to stop. He instantly turned his horse's head and galloped off. At that moment Mr Roper came up on horseback; he kindly dismounted, and giving me his horse I went away in pursuit. Near the Plough Inn a road workman was bleeding from a cut by the Captain's sword. I was well mounted, but my quarry was better mounted. Away through Westhead we went on to Ormskirk, where you may be sure the "race" aroused the greatest excitement. I reached Moor Street in time to see the Captain disappearing down Aughton Street. Here he slashed another Irishman, inflicting a nasty gash, but I had no time for his victims; I kept on the gallop, but eventually lost him in Kirkby. I learned afterwards that he had pulled up at a farmyard, and there washed the blood from his sword. I continued the search throughout the night, and the next morning I found him at a farmhouse in Lathom, tenanted by Mr Shaw. His mare - a beautiful animal - was in the stable, having thrown all her shoes and showing evidence of the hard ride. The Captain was upstairs, and as I was ascending he came to the landing and cried pleasantly: "All right, officer! I'm your prisoner."

When I took him into custody he smilingly said: "I would have surrendered at first, but I wasn't going to have it said that you had overtaken my darling Polly" (his mare). he had that day ridden one hundred miles without dismounting, and he had had the mare out with him in India, where he was supposed to have had a sunstroke which at times affected hi mind. He, however, was commited for trial at the Assizes, and two members of old Lancashire families were bail for his appearance. Edwin James, who had a great name in those days, was with other leading counsel briefed for the defence. Indeed, they had secured the "talent" much to the disgust of the magistrates' clerk, who wanted to brief counsel for the prosecution. He, however, was told that there was a young fellow named Jack Holker, a Manchester man, who looked like being a "fighter", and he briefed him.

The prosecution consented to the charges being reduced to misdemenour, where upon the defending counsel asked that prisoner might be allowed to sit in the Court and not to enter the dock. Lord James Willes refused, saying that there must be no distinction made between the rich and the poor, and that answer has often been quoted in Police Courts. The sentence was fine of £500 and three months at a first class misdemeanant in Lancaster Castle.

The Captain must have been suffering from some strange aberration of mind at the time, for he was usually the most gentlemanly and kind-hearted of men, and the persons he wounded were handsomly compensated by his family.

Edwin James, who figured in that case, soon afterwards went to America. Jack Holker became Lord Justice Holker. The magistrates' clerk used to say that it was our case which made him.

CHAPTER FIVE

In 1864 I was appointed superintendent of the Bacup and Rossendale Division. Rossendale at that time had the reputation of being one of the wealthiest valleys in England. Nearly all the manufacturers were self-made men, whose education had been snatched in the few short hours they had to spare from toil, and whose good natural qualities, backed by real English tenacity of purpose and dogged perseverance, put them into commanding positions. Yet as they "got on" they kept their simplicity of character; there was no "side" about them; they were really good natured, hearty and breezy. Still, with increasing means there naturally came in better ways of living, accompanied by luxuries unheard of in a previous generation. There were folks, too, who were conservative in their ideas, and who had notions as to what was right and proper. Fourteen years previously, in 1850, one of the largest tradesmen in Bury, a town with 50,000 of a population, bought a piano for his daughters. The neighbours were aghast. "The idea," they murmured; "the idea of Mr F.— getting a piano in his house!" Upon my return to the district I found that "the idea" had caught on - a great many of the factory operatives even had pianos in their houses.

Let me give an amusing instance of how trade was then booming. I was Inspector of Weights and Measures, in addition to my other appointments, and on visiting the shops one day I was told that an old woman who kept a small shop had received her first dividend from a co-operative mill which had not been opened very long. A neighbour, who was also a shareholder, had brought it for her. "Howd yohr apron!" he ordered her, and obeying she threw the money into her lap. The old lady looked astonished and bewildered. "Why, whatever hasta done?" she exclaimed. "Aw didn't want me brass back; Aw nobbut wanted mi divi." And she had only got her dividend. It amounted to 70 per cent!

CHRONICLES OF A VICTORIAN DETECTIVE

Just a little experience of my own. The rattle of the machinery in a cotton mill near where I was used to grate on my ears until I bought a few shares in the concern. The dividend was 25 per cent. The machinery ceased to rattle; its music was as sweet to me as that of the harp.

Yet, notwithstanding the increase in material prosperity in those early days, the largest tradesmen were satisfied to live in the back parlours of their shops. Now, and for a good many years past, this class live far from their business, in the suburbs, in handsome substantial villas. Splendour and grandeur are not always unequivocal evidences of prosperity, but it is safe to say that so far as the majority of Lancashire manufacturers are concerned, they are not illustrative of the proverb that "All is not gold that glitters." Their success is undoubted, and in them is reflected the general prosperity of the county, due largely to well-directed perseverance and energy.

Between Bacup and Burnley - a distance of seven miles - the road was rather a lonely one, and there were frequent reports of pedestrians travelling along it having been attacked and robbed. A short time after I had been in the district, the Court business at Bacup having ended, several of the magistrates remained discussing these reports. I said: "Well, I'll alter this state of affairs if the devil isn't in it; and if he is in it - I'll alter it." I took the matter in hand at once. I established meeting points, and midway between the two towns my men from the surrounding villages met at midnight. I myself attended there two or three nights a week. On one occasion I encountered two men on the road. They stopped in front of me. "We are hard up," said one; "what have you got for us?" I answered them rather gruffly, and walked slowly on, bracing myself for an emergency. I always carried at night a good strong oak stick, facetiously called "Clear the kitchen", and I had it well gripped. But they hung back, and I distinctly heard one call the other a coward. The attack that I expected failed, and to tell the truth I was disappointed. A week or so afterwards a man came early one morning to report that a farmhouse just off this road had been entered, and clothing, etc., stolen. I sent men out upon the different roads. I had a fast-trotting cob, which I put into a drag, and accompanied by my groom we drove rapidly towards Burnley.

Just as we were entering the town I caught sight of two men, carrying bundles. I recognised them as the two men who had previously stopped me on the road. They made a slight resistance, but they were taken into custody, the case was clearly proved against them, they turned out to be old offenders, and they were each sentenced to fifteen years penal servitude.

A cotton mill on the Todmorden road had frequently been robbed, and we found in the course of our enquiries that after each robbery carts from Todmorden were seen on the road. It came as an inspiration to me that here might be cause and effect. There was, of course, nothing unusual in vehicles travelling on the highway late at night or early in the morning for perfectly legitimate purposes, but here the thefts were of so extensive a nature that they indicated that there must be some means of getting away the booty other than carrying on the person. A detective must try theories improbable as well as probable to the "lay" mind, and it came into my head that these carts might have something to do with the thefts, and that the proceeds were being conveyed into Todmorden in this way. I went over to the town, and the thought turned out splendidly. I found a quantity of the stolen goods in the possession of men who were connected, in a small way, with the cotton trade itself. They were convicted at the Preston Quarter Sessions, and sentenced to long terms of imprisonment.

I spent a very happy time at Bacup, but my station was damp - the quartering of the police in those days did not receive the case it does today - I applied for a transfer to Lancaster, and the application was granted. The magistrates, court officials, and solicitors were kind enough to make complimentary references to my services, and the "Bacup Times," in its issue of the 29th September, 1886, said: - "It is with great regret that we announce the removal from our town of Richard Jervis, Esq., Superintendent of Police. Mr Jervis has applied for removal to a drier part of the county. Consequently he removes to Lancaster tomorrow, 30th inst. We are sure Mr. Jervis, in leaving us, is followed by the good wishes of all classes of the inhabitants of the district. During the two years or rather more which he has resided here he has frequently been complimented by the Bench for the impartial manner in which he has brought cases before them. Not unfrequently have we heard the prisoners speak in praise of him whilst his men who have done duty under him regret his removal very much."

CHRONICLES OF A VICTORIAN DETECTIVE

The "Bacup News" declared: — "Personally we have great pleasure in bearing testimony to his worth, both as a public servant and as a gentleman. It is with regret we announce his departure from amongst us, and only hope that his successor will endeavour to follow the excellent example in conduct that his predecessor has left him."

On the 1st October, 1866, I took charge of the Lancaster Division. Before I entered upon my duties, Capt. Elgie, the Chief Constable of the County, informed me that robberies were numerous and detections few. The crimes' book amply bore out his statement. Farmhouses were entered, poultry houses were frequently raided, poaching was so rife and so successful a business that scarcely a head of game could be got from the preserves by their lawful owners. I first put the police force into order, and then I organised a system of surveillance and supervision of all roads, and farm and landed property. In a very short time we broke up whole gangs of thieves and poachers. Several of the worst characters were sent to long terms of imprisonment, crime decreased at least 50 per cent., and the game preserves became so 'preserved' that where once there was no sport the shooting parties began to make big bags.

That Northern Division is a very picturesque part of the county. On the one side the Pennine Range of Yorkshire opens out to view; on the other the Cumbrian Group delights the view of the beholder. But the beauties of the district were often marred by crime and that of a varied character. On the highroad passing through the division north and south now and then rather serious felonies were committed by tramps. We were, however, very fortunate in getting hold of some of them, and the exemplary punishment meted out to them tended greatly to improve the safety of peaceful and law-abiding dwellers upon that road.

At one time an outbreak of the cattle plague under mysterious and suspicious circumstances not only inflicted great loss upon farmer, but gave a vast amount of trouble to the police in tracing its origin; and perhaps of all the officers, Sergeant Cross, now the Superintendent of the Seaforth Division, was the most harassed. He had charge of the Hornby section, and he worked indefatigably day and night for weeks in investigating the matter. So arduous were his exertions that his health was

39

threatened, but still he persevered, and finally he ran the delinquent to earth - a gentleman farmer, who held a large farm on the borders of Westmorland. This man was summoned for not giving notice to the police that he had an ox suffering from pleuro-pneumonia on his premises. Three months previously he had bought twenty three oxen, and subsequently defendant, noticing that one of the animals was suffering from this disease, instead of notifying the police, sent his brother to Preston to dispose of the remainder of the stock, which was about the easiest way of spreading an epidemic that could be devised. The defendant was fined £5 and costs.

At the next Hornby Petty Sessions the same defendant was summoned upon two similar charges. He had been actuated by the most selfish motives; the disease had extended from his home premises to those of a neighbour, Mr Faulkner, who had actually warned him that such a thing was likely to happen. The defendant could set up no plea of ignorance of the law; he had, indeed, tried to set it at defiance, but the cases were clearly proved against him, among the veterinary surgeons I called for the police being Professor Bell, of Carlisle. I suggested to the Bench that imprisonment without the option of a fine would best fit the offence, and the Bench, promising to adopt this course on the next appearance of the party, were content to impose a penalty of £20 and costs in each case, and the fines and costs amounted to £63. 8s. 1d. The defendant's punishment did not end there. Mr Faulkner brought an action for damages against him at the Appleby Assizes through defendant's negligence. Sergeant Cross and I were subpoened on behalf of the plaintiff, and he obtained a verdict, so that altogether the defendant paid dearly for his defiance of the law.

The local Press took up the matter in their editorial columns and the result of the prosecutions was that farmers exercised greater care in observing the regulations as to cattle diseases and in preventing the spread of contagion to other stocks.

In many parts of the county where I have been stationed reports of robberies have been made to me which proved on investigation to have been no robberies at all, but pure imaginative flights of the mind, made for various reasons. In some instances men, chiefly in manufacturing districts, weaved these romances in order to deceive their wives or parents.

CHRONICLES OF A VICTORIAN DETECTIVE

They had been in bad company and got relieved of their money. This had to be counted for at home; they tore and soiled their clothing, scratched themselves, and made up stories of having been assaulted and robbed on the highway. In several cases we were able to prove that the money had been lost by gambling and in other questionable ways.

Here is a little piece of imagination by a servant girl employed by a farmer at Quernmore. She had come home one Thursday night at a rather later hour than was allowed to her, splashed with mud and bearing other evidence of ill-usage. She said she had been waylaid by two bad men, and who assaulted and robbed her. I sent for the girl to my office. I closely questioned her. Owing to the darkness she could give no clue as to the identification of the men, but she asserted that they had robbed her of a pair of clogs and some linen which she had bought at Lancaster, from whom she could not say. I promised to find out for her, and then she magnanimously asked me to bother no more about the case. I told her that I must - for her sake as well as others. She began to answer my questions at random and wildly. She contradicted herself over and over again, and I knew she was lying. Finally she confessed that the whole adventure was a fiction. "No followers" were allowed at her place, she had been "sweethearting" rather too long on that night, and she accounted for her late hours by inventing that beautiful story.

Here is another instance of precocity in imaginative effort. The fourteen year old son of a farmer at Tatham, left to "mind" the house on Sunday night, on the return of his father told a dreadful story. A man, about 5ft 5in in height, dressed in dark clothes, his face covered with crape, entered the house, and under threats of murder compelled the lad to show him where the money was. The robber broke open a chest of drawers and stole a £5 note, a silver watch, and other articles and left the house. I was called to the house. I heard the father in silence, and then I said to Sergeant Cross, who had accompanied me: "Lock this boy up!" It was too much for the lad. He confessed that he had himself taken the note and watch, and changed the former at Bentham. He produced the money. More than that, he confessed to having a few weeks previously broken into Tatham Schools. The poor father's face was a study during these revelations. He, simple, honest soul, could not conceive that there could be such depths of duplicity in a child, and he was terribly distressed over the occurrence.

41

CHAPTER SIX

A GIRL'S TALE OF TERROR-AN ACCOMPLISHED ROGUE-
THE NETHERBY HALL GANG-A WOMAN FORGER-
THE MURDERED CHILD AND THE "BLACK MUFF WITH WHITE SPOTS."

I have already given several instances of how necessary it is for the police to make thorough investigation into all the circumstances of cases of alleged robbery, burglary, and other crimes reported to them, the more especially if specific persons are directly implicated in the offences. Unbounded faith in human nature in its present imperfect state is a delusion and a snare to the police officer; he must ever be on his guard against the aims of malice, jealousy, and wanton recklessness. And I have always striven, and make it a point, to impress upon the men of my division that it was as much their duty to disclose all the facts they learned which made for the innocence of prisoners as it was also their duty to give evidence which tended to prove their guilt.

Here is a case illustrative of the necessity of acting upon that principle. About thirty-five years ago a report came to my office late one night that the Vicarage at Yealand Conyers had been entered during the temporary absence of the Vicar, the Rev T. S Shaw, and his wife, and that the domestic servant, who was alone, had been stabbed. I at once drove over to the place, which is about nine miles north of Lancaster, and is said to be one of the prettiest villages in England. The servant was lying upon a couch in the dining-room, and among several local gentlemen present was the doctor, who described the wound as serious but not dangerous. The young woman's story was that in attempting to stop the man who had entered the house in the act of carrying off some silver articles he stabbed her. She gave a full description of him, and acting upon that the police that very night arrested a pedlar in Silverdale, a village two or three miles away. he exactly answered the description, and he had been seen going to the Vicarage at the time specified, but I was very soon satisfied from his

CHRONICLES OF A VICTORIAN DETECTIVE

Somewhat of a scene took place next morning in the Court at Lancaster Castle. Although the young woman swore that the pedlar was the man who had stabbed her, I told the Bench that I was satisfied in my own mind that he was innocent, and I asked for his discharge. Mrs Shaw, the girl's mistress, was indignant. She loudly protested against his discharge; she was positive he was the man. She had dreamt that very night that she saw the girl stabbed by the man in the dock! This, however, did not convince the magistrates, and the prisoner was set at liberty. During the day I again visited the Vicarage, and found the Vicar with three or four other gentlemen of the district engaged in the delightful task of drafting a letter to the Home Secretary complaining about my wicked conduct in procuring the discharge of a man who had been so clearly identified as a villain. I asked them to wait a day or two before they posted the letter, and no doubt inwardly wondering what I was "up to" they consented, but it was after the manner of men who knew that there was no hope for me, and that they were only delaying my punishment.

The following morning I drove once more to the Vicarage, and requested a private interview with the servant. The Vicar and his wife were up in arms against it. "Very well," I said with an air of indifference, "in that case she goes with me in that dog-cart to Lancaster." They stared and gasped and gave way.

The girl appeared, pale and agitated. I took out my watch, and eyeing her sternly I said: " I am giving you three minutes and no longer to tell me the truth." She wished that all kinds of awful things might happen to her if she had not told the truth. "You have just half a minute left," I said, "in which to say whether I have to have the truth or you go with me." She broke down. She cried bitterly. "Oh ! sir," she sobbed, "will you forgive me if I tell you the truth ?" "Wait !" I ordered her, and rang the bell for Mr and Mrs Shaw. They listened confounded and amazed by the girl's miserable confession. She had inflicted the wound upon herself with a potato knife, which she had buried at the bottom of the garden and was found with blood on it; and she had concocted all the rest, dragging in a description of the poor pedlar as that of her assailant. And what do you think was her motive ? Merely that she did not like to be left alone in the house, and that she thought by this story she would never be left alone again! And to gratify that silly whim here was a poor man most monstrously dragged in as a culprit, certain had he been sent for trial, to have been sentenced to penal servitude.

I could give numerous instances of the folly of striking up acquaintance among strangers, particularly with those one sometimes meets with on the railway or in hotels.

I "took" a clever swindler who had a number of aliases. He was smart and intelligent, and was a master in roguery. Sometimes he posed as a traveller; at other times he advertised alluring appointments in the colonies, and accepted all applicants who could pay the necessary "fees". Thus furnished with money he lived well at hotels, and from them upon his printed notepaper he drew many a goodly fish from the ocean of credulity. He had the audacity to advertise "the lucrative post of Natal Secretary", and letters from applicants were found in his possession. He had obtained deposits upon the sale of property which existed only in his imagination; he secured pre-paid advertisements which never appeared; he obtained 30s from a gentleman at Shipley "on account of expenses he had incurred by his father, who was seriously ill", but the father was well and hearty and knew nothing of the rascal; he opened a shop at Scarborough, and "let in" manufacturers right and left, "doing" one firm at Leeds to the extent of £50. I found the addresses of about 200 persons upon this accomplished shark, and singular enough one address was that of my brother at St Helens. Prisoner had got hold of it in this way. At the Royal Hotel, Manchester, he met a young gentleman named Mr Blackwell, of Kenilworth, and in conversation Mr Blackwell not only told where he resided, but mentioned that he was going to spend the Sunday with Mr Jervis. The very next day the scamp posted off to Kenilworth and informed Mr and Mrs Blackwell that their son had been knocked down by an omnibus in Manchester, and was lying seriously injured at the Royal Hotel. The young gentleman's sister accompanied the swindler back by train, but at Crewe he got out for a few moments, and on returning he informed Miss Blackwell that he had met a gentleman to whom he owed an account, and "would she kindly lend him £10 until they got to Manchester, when he would make it all right?" She lent him the money, and the man vanished for good until I arrested him. Mr Blackwell's accident was, of course, a fabrication. The man had been previously convicted, and his last sentence was one of fifteen years penal servitude.

That the motto, "Be careful of your company," is a sound one to follow when among strangers may be further illustrated by the following incidents. A few years ago I had in custody three men for the theft of £100 from a public-house in Ormskirk. They were part of a body of scoundrels known as "The Netherby Hall gang"—one of two of whom a short time previously had been hanged at Carlisle for murder in resisting arrest for burglary at Netherby Hall. Now a North Country Solicitor who had defended some of them in different parts of the country, and who was asked to defend my trio at Ormskirk, told me that some months ago he saw two of them in a Preston hotel, chatting in a very free and friendly manner with several of the most influential gentlemen of the town. They started slightly on the appearance of the solicitor, and gave him a look accompanied by a gesture which conveyed a threat of violence if he "gave them away." One of the gentlemen was so taken up with them that he invited them to dine at his house on the following night, and the consequences might have been serious to the inconsiderate inviter had he not been warned of the true character of the men he had too hastily taken into his confidence. Agreeable manners are the stock-in-trade of many a rogue with which he plies his villainy among the credulous and inexperienced.

Perjury, when I first went to Lancaster, was so rife in the Police Court as to render it almost impossible for the magistrates to administer justice. It was astonishing the amount of evidence which could be brought against the police in any case, and while, of course, a policeman possessed of that human frailty which belongs to all men, is at times liable to err, it was evident in this state of affairs that there was something more than mere erring in the continual array of witnesses brought against every officer. I had to show that the police force was not composed wholly of liars, and in a very short time I had two prosecutions for perjury against men in good positions in life. Both were sentenced to eighteen months' imprisonment, and for a time, at any rate, perjury was sensibly checked in the Police Court.

A number of forged bank notes of the Lancaster Banking Company—at least a dozen of them—had been passed in the division. We were handicapped in our efforts to trace the culprits by the fact that we were not notified as speedily as we should have been of the uttering of the notes. In nearly every instance they had been passed on publicans in payment for a small bottle of brandy. I sent a notice to all the publicans to be specially on their guards against the practice, and one night Mr Holmes, a licensed victualler of Morecambe, came to the office with a forged note he had taken an hour or so before from a woman. Suspecting that she would be leaving the town by train I hurried to the Castle Station accompanied by a sergeant. We saw a woman who answered the description given to me, waiting on the platform for a Preston train, and she was taken into custody. On the way to the police station she tried every artifice to obtain the use of her hands, to remove, as it seemed to me, something from under her skirts. But we did not allow this liberty, and at the office I instructed the female searcher to make a most careful examination of the prisoner's clothing. She reported that she had done so, and had found no banknotes. I directed that the whole of her clothing should be taken from her, and the result was that £5 forged notes were found concealed on her person. Subsequently, from information she gave, a sergeant went over to Preston, and there in a couple of rooms taken by the prisoner were found a camera and all the necessary appliances for photography, together with a couple of negatives—facsimiles of forged notes. These had been pasted together in halves in order to give them the appearance of having been in circulation. In addition a number of partially prepared £5 notes were found. Prisoner at the Assizes pleaded guilty to the charge of forging and uttering, and was sentenced to ten years' penal servitude.

Of "Smashers," that is, utterers of counterfeit coin, I have had numerous cases. The first was very nearly in my career, when I was in Bury. I arrested the man from description at the railway station, but on the way to the police office he managed to get rid of several base half crowns. That was a lesson to me, teaching me the necessity of either searching prisoners on the spot, or of securing their hands. At Lancaster I had half-a-dozen or more of these cases. In one instance where a man and woman were apprehended, the latter had underneath her clothes and under her left armpit artfully concealed a bag which contained 17 base florins and 43 base shillings. They were each sentenced to eighteen months, with hard labour.

In the eleven years I was at Lancaster I had three committals to the Assizes on the capital charge, but in two of them verdicts of manslaughter were returned. The third case was one which caused considerable excitement in the district. On the 15th November, 1872, while attending the Petty Sessions of Lancaster Castle, I was informed that on the previous day a woman, a stranger, had been seen going along the footpath in the direction of Aldcliffe, leading a little girl by the hand, and that about an hour afterward she returned— alone. I sent a couple of sergeants to search the pit and ponds in the neighbourhood, and the next day, Sunday, they found the body of the child referred to in one of the ponds.

The only description we had of the woman was that she was of dark complexion, that she was carrying a black muff with white spots upon it. Even this information, meagre as it was, was only gleaned from a girl nine years of age, and it did not seem to be very encouraging. But trifles are not to be scorned, and that muff was destined to play an important part in that most exciting of all hunts, the hunt of a human being. "A black muff with white spots." I could not get it out of my mind; I inquired for it everywhere, and by and by— after five days' search — I came across a publican who had travelled by train from Lancaster to Carnforth on the afternoon of the day of the murder, and he remembered travelling in the same compartment with a woman who had a black muff with white spots. There seemed to be a sinister attraction about that muff. He remembered it well. But he was hazy about the woman herself, and yet he had an idea that she had booked to Carlisle. I telegraphed and wrote to the Carlisle police. I waited two days, and still no answer. I was impatient, and went over to Carlisle, determining upon as near a house to house enquiry as possible, in streets in which I thought it likely that persons of the servant class could obtain lodgings. For the idea was fixed in my mind that the woman I wanted was a domestic servant travelling North on her holidays. After eight or ten hours' exhausting search the fatal black muff with white spots reappeared. I found a house where a woman with that article had lodged for a week, from the night of the 15th November. Moreover, the landlady had noticed—(bless her inquisitive eyes !)—that she had written to a "Mr Gresty, Northenden, near Stockport." I had finished with

CHRONICLES OF A VICTORIAN DETECTIVE

Carlisle. I caught the Manchester express, and reached Northenden by midnight. The police-constable of the village showed me the house at which the man named Gresty lived, and in the porch of the church which stood opposite that dwelling I kept watch until seven o'clock the next morning. Then I saw the bedroom blind drawn up by a woman, and a few minutes afterwards the front door was opened. I ran across and entered without ceremony. Gresty and his wife were on the stairs. I told them I wanted to see a young woman who was staying there. Both barred the way, and the man said: "You cant come up these stairs; this is a private house." At that moment I heard shuffling in the room above; I pushed the two aside, and I entered the bedroom. On the dressing table was that ominous black muff with white spots. The woman was dressing. I charged her with the murder. She denied the charge or that she had ever seen the child. Mrs groves, the wife of a brewer near Northenden, in whose service she was, was ignorant of the fact that prisoner had had a child, but she gave me the address of a person in Manchester upon whom prisoner called when it was her afternoon off. There I found the woman who had brought up the child from a baby, and who, on learning of its cruel fate, was upset, and repeatedly sobbed: "My dear little Carrie !" The prisoner had taken the child ostensibly for a little holiday, and had written from Carlisle to say that she was leaving "Carrie" with her relatives in that town.

The prisoner was found guilty and sentenced to be hanged by Mr Justice Archibald, who stigmatised the crime as one which displayed an absence of every womanly feeling and instinct. He held out no hope of mercy for her, notwithstanding the jury's recommendation; but the humanitarians bestirred themselves on her behalf, and the night before the morning fixed for the execution she was reprieved and the sentence commuted to one of penal servitude for life.

Mr E Dawson, chairman of the Lancaster County Bench, was pleased on behalf of himself and his brother magistrates to express publicly their appreciation of my services in this case.

CHAPTER SEVEN

CHANGES IN NORTH LANCASHIRE—THE PRICE OF A COTTAGE
—JEALOUSIES AMONG THE POLICE—WATERLOO COURSING MEETING
—THE POLICE MAKE A FINE "BAG," AND CLEAR THE COURSE OF RASCALS.

About a year before I left Lancaster, Cockerham Church was broken into, and in addition to the theft of several articles some damage was done. A description was given of two men who had been seen in the neighbourhood, and a night or two afterwards I arrested two men who seemed to answer to answer that description. The evidence against them was purely circumstantial, but upon it Mr Justice Mellor sentenced them to four years' penal servitude. Upon this one of the prisoners called out: "You old ——; I'll do for you when I come out !" Whereupon the judge said: "For the threat to myself I call upon you to find two sureties in £100 each and yourself in £200 to keep the peace for two years, or in default you remain in goal during that period."

Only a few days afterwards I received a letter from that very prisoner describing where he and his mate had hidden the silver stolen from the church, and asking me to use my influence and have the bail set aside; and that, I believe, was done.

On the 1st October, 1877, I yielded up my superintendentship of the South Lonsdale Division to enter upon similar duties at Ormskirk. I had spent eleven years there not without many a moving incident and adventure, and not, I hope, without adding to my store of experience, which, rightly applied, makes a man worthier of his avocation whatever it may be. the press and the magistracy cheered and heartened me by the compliments they paid to my past service and the good wishes they expressed for my future.

Heigho ! Much of what was then my future now also lies behind me as the past, with memories only of what has been, full of changes, some sad, others cheering as evidences of progress and advancement. Lancaster itself has grown. In 1866 the population was about 13,000, and it had stood at that figure for generations. But the energy and perseverance of Mr James Williamson, now Lord Ashton, and the Messrs. Storey, keen with commercial instinct and enterprise, woke up the old county town, created work for thousands of people and helped very largely to raise the population to upwards 40,000; and Morecambe and Heysham, which were also in my division, have grown in something like the same proportion. Land values advance as the tide of industrial and residential growth sweep over a place. Let me give an illustration. A farm at the west end of Morecambe was in my early days there offered for sale at is 3d a yard. A friend of mine, who obtained a portion of it, strongly advised me to risk a purchase. I had not the eye of a prophet; I hesitated and was lost—just like my luck ! Not more than two or three years afterwards the price of the land jumped up to a guinea a yard, and now quite a town stands upon the site of that old farm. Yet I have seen much more rapid advances in building land in Lancashire during the last fifty years. At Barrow-in-Furness I had a friend who was interested in a cottage which sold for £150. It subsequently changed hands rapidly, and each purchaser made a decent profit out of his transaction, until finally the Council found that the cottage must be brought in order that they might carry out certain improvements. But they could not agree with the owner as to the price, and the question was referred to arbitration. The Court met at the Palatine Hotel, Manchester, and the Corporation triumphed. They got the cottage at a cost of upwards of £15,000 !

Thus casting my eye backward over thirty years I see many signs of increased material prosperity, and yet, alas! I find many who have fallen by the way in the march of time. There is not a single magistrate now living who was on the Ormskirk Bench thirty years ago. Taking the whole of the county there is not one left who was on the Commission of the Peace when I first entered the police service-fifty eight years ago.

After an absence of a little more than thirteen years I returned to Ormskirk, finding that the magistrates, without my knowledge, had petitioned headquarters for my return.

On my first visit to Birkdale, after entering the Division, I was somewhat startled to see placards issued by Southport asking the Birkdale people to amalgamate with that township, and one of the arguments they set forth in its favour was that Birkdale would have the advantage of being policed by Southport instead of by the County, which then furnished a sergeant and five or six constables. A deputation from the Birkdale Local Board waited upon me in reference to that particular question, and subsequently I saw the chairman of the Board, Mr Isherwood, and informed him that we were about to make some alterations in the police arrangements for the town, and that when that was done a house would be taken at Birkdale Common and an officer would be stationed there. In these and other ways I expressed myself certain that they would be satisfied with the efficient policing of the district. I applied for Sergeant Cross, whom I had left in the Lancaster Division, to be appointed the first inspector at Birkdale. This was done, and very soon afterwards a police station with cells was erected in Kent Road. Up to this time prisoners had been taken to Southport. And in course of time I was instrumental in getting the present handsome building in Weld Road, with offices and Courtroom, built. But our efforts did not altogether repress the spirit of amalgamation. Inspector Cross had not been in authority more than a couple of years or so when the question was again raised by Southport, and on this occasion handbills were sent to every house in the township asking the inhabitants to support the application. But a strong point was made of this: "That even under amalgamation Birkdale would still be policed by the County Force!" That was a point full of deep significance. The Force under new government had changed its aspect to the public; it had evidently become so popular that the proposers of amalgamation dared not touch it. The circumstance clearly shows how necessary it is for the police to do their duty without officialism, and ever bearing in mind the important fact that they are established for the protection and not the oppression of the public. Where this is duly observed they will always have the confidence and support not only of the magistrates but of the respectable portion of the community.

At that time the only station with cells in the Division was at Ormskirk; and there was only one sergeant for the Formby and Maghull sections, and he was positioned at Downholland! I succeeded in obtaining a sergeant for Formby, as well as a station with cells, and by and bye similar buildings were erected at Skelmersdale, Burscough, and Maghull, which with their appointments have helped to promote the efficiency of the Force. Yet for efficiency and economy I would like to see one police force upon similar lines to those adopted by Lord Cross in connection with the gaols.

Jealousies ought not to exist between the different police forces, because they undoubtedly affect the efficiency of a service whose object should be the guardianship of the whole country, and not merely that of a particular district. It is a good sign of the times that jealousies do not now exist to the extent they did formerly. I myself have always made it a strong point to work amicably with adjoining boroughs, and this can always be done, while at the same time we retain an excusable pride in keeping our won districts free from crime, and so far as we can drive bad characters beyond our borders. This reminds me of a joke I once had at the expense of the then Chief Constable of Lancaster, some years ago. We were walking together in Scotforth, a village adjoining the borough, and under my direct jurisdiction, when we met a notorious house-breaker, who was then living in Lancaster. I stopped him and spoke to him seriously and emphatically. I said: "Now, look here! You must go back to Lancaster. We have not room for you in the county, and I have instructed my men to run you in if you are found in our district after dusk. There are plenty of houses for you in Lancaster, and you can do as you like with them; but understand, I shall make it hot for you if we catch you in the county!" The man went away as if in deep meditation, and my companion's indignation burst forth in the astonished words: "Hang it all, Jervis, that's not fair is it?"

The Waterloo Coursing Meeting - the Mecca of all coursers and their supporters - thirty years ago was a Pandemonium. Liverpool cornermen, as well as some of the worst characters in the country, attended, with the result that assaults and robberies were the order of the day, while "welshing" ran riot. One of the favourite devices of the cowardly blackguards, who made robbery their occupation, was for a dozen of them to surround their victim, and at the time they were snatching his watch to knock him down and immediately raise the cry of "Heigh! A——-welsher!" On came the crowd, keen for slaughter, and vain were the protests of the poor innocent victim as he is being maltreated by the misguided newcomers. This and similar kinds of infamous deeds had, as I was told, been going on for ten years. Mr T.D. Hornby had been succeeded as hon. secretary by Mr Harold Brocklebank, and he gave me carte blanche in regard to the policing of the meeting. At the next "Waterloo" I increased the police, in uniform and plain clothes, by nearly thirty, and what must have excited no little wonder among the quidnuncs I took a prison van to the course.

We had a most profitable time of it; we improved the shining hour as busily as any bee could have done, and very early in the day we had taken upwards of thirty suspicious characters, and lodged them in a farm building, where we kept them until the coursing had finished for the day. They were a variegated lot, were the captives, and they included several well-known welshers. The news of the raid quickly became one of the tit-bits on the course, and over a dozen persons who had been welshed visited the farm and inspected our collection to ascertain whether there was any acquaintance with whom it might be worth while to rub shoulders again. Recognitions in many instances were mutual, and I made these welshers and their sharpers who were clearly identified disgorge their ill-gotten gains, and over £35 pounds was returned to their victims. This sharp action, followed in some cases by prosecutions, frightened the rascals and broke up gangs of them. Previously reports of the theft of from fifteen to twenty watches at every meeting were common; the number fell to an odd now and then; and in the matter of the sale of cards for admission, which are half-a-crown each, things improved so much that they came to sell twenty where they had formerly only sold one - a fact not accounted for by any mere increased attendance, but by the repression of roguery and an increased attendance of respectable people who paid for their cards, while the blackguards evaded the stewards.

I extract the following from a London sporting paper of the period to show how the substitution of order for lawlessness was appreciated outside the county:- "Waterloo Coursing: The great coursing event of the season was brought to a close on Friday, when 'Snowflight' won the blue riband of the leash, 'Hornpipe' being the runner-up. There was one particular feature in connection with the meeting that should not be passed by. I allude to the excellent service rendered by Mr Superintendent Jervis, of the Ormskirk Division, and the men under his direction. In the matter of thieves, welshers, and blacklegs, who for past years have not only become a downright nuisance, but a serious danger to their victims, there was a decided change for the better. Hitherto, the evil has been allowed to run on without let or hindrance, but now everyone who has the leading coursing event of the country at heart will be right glad to perceive strenuous measures adopted by Mr Jervis for the suppression of what was really a scandal."

Mr J. Hartley Bibby succeeded Mr Harold Brocklebank as hon. secretary, and he also gave me a free hand in the matter of policing the meeting. Thus unhampered by restrictions one determined upon reform could only blame his own incompetency if he failed in that object. Laxity of police government leads to a laxity in order by letting in the rogues and vagabonds of society; but good organisation deprives them of their occupation, and honest, respectable men can then enjoy their own in peace.

CHAPTER EIGHT

A baby farming case I had at Birkdale not only caused considerable excitement locally, but the London as well as the Provincial Press gave lengthy reports. The late Mr B. Waugh, the director of the N.S.P.C.C., whom I met in Southport fifty years ago, came to consult with me, and on the strength of that case he established an office in Southport for the district.

There were three prisoners concerned—William Pearson, his wife, Elizabeth Pearson, and Mrs Brade, alias Oldfield. They were charged with the manslaughter of May Oldfield, three years of age, and Rosina Elizabeth Morris Oldfield, aged seventeen months. I conducted the prosecution. According to the evidence Mrs Brade, alias Oldfield, had been just prior to that time a widow, and she was reported to be of independent means. She showed some anxiety to get the children out of her care, and they were put out to nurse with the Pearsons. The point for the Bench was whether Mrs Brade had shown reasonable care in providing for the proper maintenance of the children. However that might be, there was ample evidence proving that they were kept day after day upon wet mattresses, without food, or at least without proper food, while their bodies and clothing were infested with vermin and maggots. In consequence of this neglect the children were reduced to mere skeletons, and at last they died—from starvation, so the doctors reported as the result of a post-mortem examination. They were insured, and on the death of May Oldfield the Pearsons received £4 Mrs Brade escaped, but the Pearsons were committed for trial and sentenced to penal servitude.

About 27 years ago occurred a railway disaster at Burscough, which will no doubt be still fresh in the memory of the older residents of the district. By a terrible mistake two passenger trains were allowed to proceed on the same line, in opposite directions, and a collision was the result, eight persons being killed and forty injured. The inquest was opened by the late Mr T W Barker, who was subsequently killed by a steam tram between Wigan and Upholland, and who was succeeded by the present Coroner, Mr S. Brighouse. I had on my own responsibility arrested the signalman in the case for criminal negligence, and the jury returned a verdict of manslaughter. Several persons injured in the accident died in the Preston Infirmary, and a Coroner's jury of that borough returned a similar verdict. The man, when brought before the Ormskirk magistrates, was defended by Mr R. Sadler, and I conducted the prosecution. Prisoner was committed for trial at the Assizes, but he was acquitted.

Some years ago the racial feeling was strong in the Lydiate district, native farm labourers expressing their antipathy to the immigration of Irish harvesters in attacks upon these men, which finally culminated in six men being locked up for attempted murder, arson, and robbery. These feuds, as may be very well imagined, aroused considerable alarm among farmers as well as labourers, their point being that the Irishmen were essential to the progress of local agriculture, and that if they were driven away their crops could not be gathered. To many of the farms the same men returned year after year, and to encourage them most of the farmers had built places for their separate accommodation, popularly known as "Paddy houses." The evidence given on the trial of the six prisoners referred to disclosed a state of things which could not be tolerated in a civilised community. The prisoners were first heard of about eleven o'clock one Saturday night, when they appeared at Mrs Haskayne's farm, Lydiate, armed with a choice selection of weapons. Searching a loft they found an Irishman named Munnigan, whom they savagely assaulted. From there they proceeded to Mr Milbourn's farm, where they found eight Irishmen asleep in the Paddy house. Bursting open the door they assaulted these men, and then went on to Mr Aindow's at Altcar, where five Irishmen were sleeping in the loft of the Paddy house. Smashing the window, they got inside, set fire to all the clothing of the poor fellows they could lay their hands on, and unable to get at the men above, who had barricaded themselves in their room, they tried to fire the door down. One of the victims had his pockets rifled of £1 5s., and several were seriously injured. The whole countryside was aroused, and the gang decamped, but

CHRONICLES OF A VICTORIAN DETECTIVE

I was able to bring forward the evidence of fifteen witnesses, or who in one way or another connected the men with the outrages. The hearing occupied ten hours at the Birkdale Police Court, and the prisoners were committed to the Assizes, where some were sent to penal servitude and the others to various terms of imprisonment. The cases had a salutary effect in stamping out terrorist methods, and though fights between English and Irish labourers may arise, after drinking bouts, as they had arisen previously, we have since then had no organised attempt to drive Irish harvesters from the district, by violence, in the manner I have described.

Thirty or forty years ago perjury was more rife in the police force courts than it is to-day, though none with any acquaintance with law business will be disposed to deny the offence does still exist—and that despite the greater educational advantages of the present day. Indeed, education, or rather elementary education, has not brought about that great reformation of morals which was promised by some of its advocates. No doubt we have sharper intellect among the mass of the people, and that education, as I have shown before, joined with the opening out of some rational ways of recreation has led to a decrease in drunkenness; but education, so far as a certain class of criminals is concerned, has helped to make them more dangerous to society. Now, perjury makes the administration of justice difficult and impossible, and in every division over which I have had charge I have watched for opportunities of putting a scotch in the wheel of this evil. I had not been very long in the Ormskirk Division before I had two or three prosecutions for the offence, and the exemplary sentences passed upon the culprits had a markedly deterrent effect.

Yet more notorious was another part of the county in this respect. It was common talk that witnesses could be bought for a few shillings, especially where they were wanted to rebut evidence brought by the police against beersellers. On one occasion we had a prosecution against a beerhouse keeper, and an important point was as to the exact time at which the offence was committed. For the defence a not particularly intelligent-looking witness was called, and he gave the time which suited the defendant's case to a minute. I asked him how he had got the time so pat, and he replied, "I looked at th' clock." I pointed to the Courtroom clock, and asked him the time. He hesitated, hummed, and hawed, and finally confessed that he could not read the figures on that timepiece !

The excitement of a general election nearly thirty years ago extended to Ormskirk. A riotous mob of 500 or 600 persons paraded the streets threatening and assaulting people who were not of their "colour," and the crowd grew when the cheerful intelligence was proclaimed that there was no law on election days. In Railway Road they besieged a building in which some inoffensive people had taken shelter from the fury of this mob, excited against them because of their "colours."

I happened to come up with half a dozen constables, and I ordered them to draw their truncheons and use them. The order was so effectually obeyed that a score or two of the mob were yelling and sprawling in all directions, broken heads not improving the harmony of their voices. Their comrades, convinced that discretion was the better part of valour, stood not upon the order of their going, but "skedaddled." That quietened the upholders of "no law," and there were no more disorders during that election.

And here let me say in regard to general elections that there is no comparison between the conduct of them at the present day and that of fifty and sixty years ago. Then for fun, excitement, and broken heads, Clitheroe and Blackburn furnished more than any other places at which I attended. Free drinks were dispensed with open hand at the public houses, bribery was unblushingly rampant, and gangs of ruffians - (hired on most occasions) - poured in from the adjoining towns, armed with heavy sticks, their objects being to terrorise opposite parties, and to shout the loudest at the hustings. Eggs of uncertain age but of decided flavour were freely levelled at the heads of opponents with other missiles, some not less disagreeable, others more calculated to make a mark and leave one. Voters were smuggled into public-houses, and kept there until they could be taken to the polling booths; there was the discordant noise of opposing bands of music, the parading of party colours through the streets, the yells of opposing clans. They were, indeed, lively times which the lowering of the Franchise and the vote by ballot have materially altered. At that time the voting power was confined to owners of freehold property, £50 householders in the county, and £20 householders in the borough.

CHRONICLES OF A VICTORIAN DETECTIVE

About the same time there arose serious colliery riots in many of the colliery districts of Lancashire. Though all the Skelmersdale pits with one exception were also affected by the strike, the men kept quiet, thanks in a great measure to the exertions of their agents, the late Mr Thomas Aspinwall, one of the most sensible of miners' agents. But the law-abiding behaviour of the colliers there was apparently not to the liking of outsiders. One colliery, the Chapel House, was working, the masters having agreed to the men's terms, and by-and-by the rumours that mobs were coming to alter this state of things grew into certainties. I make the following extract from the Liverpool Press:—"On Tuesday the police were informed that a mob of several hundred men had left Wigan for Skelmersdale. Thirty constables, under Superintendent Jervis, armed with cutlasses, met them at Tawd Bridge, on the boundary of the township, and found them armed with cudgels and other weapons. they were disarmed and then allowed to proceed on the assurance that they were only going to attend a meeting, and that they had no attention of breaking the law. The Superintendent of Wigan had followed the mob with twenty constables. One-half of the mob went towards the Chapel House Colliery, and Mr Jervis followed them with one-half of his men. The mob increased in numbers and violence. Stones were thrown, and the Wigan Superintendent and several constables were more or less injured. The police charged the rioters with their truncheons, and they then made off in the direction of Wigan as fast as they could. The public-houses in the town were visited by the police, and persons who were believed to belong to the mob were turned out and driven towards Wigan. Many of the mob received injuries which they will not soon forget."

As a result of this riot, a man named John Molyneux, of Wigan, was brought up, charged with being a ringleader in the affair. He told me a curious story. He said that he would have been at Skelmersdale had not the landlord of an inn there been previously to Wigan, and after "standing" five or six of ale for him and a number of his mates informed them that there was to be a meeting at Skelmersdale, and that if they would come he would "stand" them two barrels of beer.

Sufficient evidence was obtained to convict the prisoner, and he received a long term of imprisonment.

CHAPTER NINE

Twenty years ago Bolton was the scene of serious disturbances arising out of an extensive strike of workers. For three months I was posted there in charge of a force of 200men. But this not being deemed sufficient, an application was made for the military. Now I had among my men a number of good horsemen, some of whom had served with crack cavalry regiments, and I suggested to the Mayor, the town Clerk, and the Borough Chief Constable, Mr Holgate, that if they would supply me with from fifteen to twenty horses I could mount them effectively, and might thus be able to keep the soldiers out, as well as save the town from additional expense and prevent the adding of any more fuel to the fire of excitement which raged in the town. The suggestion was accepted, and it worked very satisfactorily. The well-mounted, disciplined man who knows his business is invaluable where large bodies of men are agitation. He can be put more quickly on the scene of disturbance than his brother on foot, and he can break up and disperse a crows better. So it was in this case. Folks who don't mind risking a tussle with the police, foot to foot, do not care to have their corns "touched" by the iron heels of the horse, and they will give way handy enough when it is a case of "by your leave or without it." I had a fine charger placed at my command, and some of my men were well mounted. We were kept busy enough. Serious damage had been done to some of the large foundries; more was threatened to others. Hence a number of my men were permanently posted at some of the works; a Mounted Force was engaged in guarding "knobsticks" to and from their work; while I had always a number of men on reserve at the Town Hall, and these were frequently called out to quell disturbances. Some compensation to the weary and often dangerous work of the police in these circumstances was found in the generous manner in which they were treated by the Town Council and the foundry masters at whose works they were posted.

After the first two or three weeks we got affairs pretty well in hand, and

CHRONICLES OF A VICTORIAN DETECTIVE

quarters were provided for me at an hotel near the Town Hall. When one has for over thirty years made the hunting of men the chief business of his life, his weakness is, when thrown among strangers, to try to "weigh them up" to ascertain whether every one has anything beyond the face value he sets before you. Now among the "commercials" at this hotel I noticed one especially. He looked gold, but to me he did not ring true. He seemed to pass most of the time playing the piano and singing psalms. Don't set me down as a sceptic, but I am always suspicious of a man who parades the religious spirit, especially in a hotel. I hinted to the proprietor that, like the Scot, I had "ma doots" about the man. He looked at me quizzically and smiled. "Ah, you policemen," he said, "you see a swindler in every man you don't know. You've got into that way. But, bless you, sir he's all right." I turned from him to cultivate an acquaintance with my "suspect." I was interested to learn that he lived in Lancaster, and I asked him who were his friends there. He gave me two names—one that of the chaplain of the Castle, and the other that of a magistrate and a visiting justice at the Castle ! Strange that his acquaintance should be confined to castle folk, very estimable in themselves, but from the nature of their official duties apt to lead a suspicious man like myself to think that their "friend" who has no others on his visiting list has indeed been "confined." The next day I missed my man, but the proprietor again laughed off the gloomy foreboding I expressed in regard to him. The following day he was still missing; but the beautiful confidence of that hotel keeper could not be shaken. I suggested that his portmanteau should be broken open, for which I would take full responsibility, and my persistence had its reward. The trunk was opened; it contained three good-sized bricks ! My friend, the proprietor, was crestfallen. I circulated the man's description, and he was arrested, I believe in Accrington for similar offences. He was wanted at other places for fraud, and it turned out that he had served a year in Lancaster Gaol. Hence his acquaintance with the chaplain and the visiting justice !

In these reminiscences I do not pretend to follow any particular order. I have jotted down in my note-book many things as they have occurred to me which really lie outside my official duties, and I have just come across some memoranda respecting the characteristics of the Lancashire dialect as I have observed it in my peregrinations through the county. In my opinion the purest dialect as a dialect is spoken in East Lancashire. One thing, however, which has struck me is the variance in the vocabulary. In no two places is it exactly alike, so that I have never experienced any difficulty in locating the habitat of a Lancashire factory operative when away from home. Let me give an instance. Some years ago I was in St. James's Park, London, with my wife and daughter, watching the birds on a lake. Near at hand-a-dozen Lancashire trippers, who were speaking unreservedly in the well-known "twang" of Bury and Rossendale. I listened to them for a few moments, and then said in a voice that would reach them: "I wonder whether there are any Bury and Rossendale folk in London now ?" The men looked and stared "Eh, I'se fra Bury !" cried one; "And I'se fra Rawtenstaw !" exclaimed another. It was a very hot day, and their wives were seated on the grass. "Eh, sithee ! shouted one of the men, "here's a fella' knows Bury and Rossenda' !" Up jumped the woman and surrounded me— to the great amusement of a party of ladies and gentlemen who were standing near-to view close at hand the great curiosity of a man who knew their homes so far away.

But though Lancashire men may differ in their dialect my experience leads me to say of them as it is said of a well-known advertised tea that they are all "good." The nicknames which the inhabitants of some towns bear are curious. We have "Bowton Trotters," "Bury Roughs," "Owdham Roughyeds," Liverpool "gentlemen," and Manchester "men."

Many years ago I made the acquaintance of Mr. Thos. Newbigging at Bacup, who has made a study of the character and dialect of the people of East Lancashire, and who has often regaled me with stories of Lancashire humour. He told me one concerning an Oldham chap who was sent to Preston Gaol. He was put upon the treadmill, and by-and-bye the exercise made his back and legs ache. Turning to one of the turnkeys he groaned: "Bi gum, owd mon, if this devil had bin i' Owdham they'd ha' turned it bi pawer afoor neaw !"

Another "Owdhamer" was at a cricket match, when he saw a pickpocket caught by the police. Nodding towards the thief, he remarked dryly to a friend: "Sharp as thoose chaps are they'd have a job to ta' ma brass. Aw'll tell thee what Aw do. When Aw comes here Aw sticks mi brass reet deawn at th' bottom o' mi treauser's pocket, an' then Aw puts abeaut half a pint o' nuts at th' top on't; it ta'es some scrawpin' eaut, Aw con tell thee !"

Pigeon flying is a pastime greatly beloved of the colliers, as anyone may readily discover at Wigan and Skelmersdale, and the following story is told of an ardent and hardened pigeon flyer: He lay sick unto death, and he was visited by a parson, who sought to prepare him for his last journey, and who painted in vivid colours the joy of the angels in heaven. The sick man was very much interested. "And shall Aw really ha' wings when Aw get to heaven ?" he asked half-hopefully, half incredulously. "Oh ! yes," was the reply. "And will yoh ha' wings too, when yoh get theer ?" asked the collier eagerly. "To be sure," replied the clergyman. "We shall all have wings." The sick man feebly grasped his hand and looked earnestly upon him. "Well, nah, con we mak' a bargain ?" he asked. "When tha comes up yon Aw'll fly thee for five bob !"

The first Bishop of Manchester, Dr Fraser, was one day on the outskirts of that city, when he came across two gutter lads who were busy making what appeared to be a mud house. He spoke to them in characteristic fashion, and inquired what they were doing. "We've been makin' a church." "Oh !-Ah !-I see !" said the Bishop, very much amused. "Very good. I see here is the entrance, this is the nave, here are the aisles, there the pews, and—Yes !-here is the pulpit. But, my smart little fellows, where is the parson ?" "Oh ! we have not getten muck enough to mak' a passon !" was the disconcerting reply.

A new vicar who was going to Bolton asked his way of a lad who was weeding turnips in a field. "Well," said the boy readily, "yoh mun goo across yon bleach croft and into th' loan, and yoh'll get a Doffcocker, and then yoh're in the hee-road, and yoh con goo straight on." The vicar thanked him, and asked the nature of his duties. "Oh ! Aw cleeans up th' shippon," was the reply, "pills pratoes, run arrants, and other odd jobs. And if Aw may be so bowd, win yoh tell me what yoh do for a livin' ?" "I am a minister of the Gospel," said the vicar. The lad stared. "But what dun yoh do ?" he persisted. "I preach and teach the way to heaven," explained the other. The boy gave him a droll look and shook his head.

"Nay, nay," he said, "dunnot yoh pretend to teach me th' road to heaven and yoh dunnot know th' road to Bowton !"

A well-known who was playing for a few nights at Wigan was fond of telling the following as an actual incident he experienced in that district. He entered the room of a public-house at Upholland, in which were some colliers. One was in great trouble, having lost his youngest boy, and his companions were trying to comfort him. "It's hard to bear, Aw know, Jack," said one, "but tha mun cheer up, mon, an mak' th' best of a bad job."

But the bereaved father would not be comforted. "Eh ! yoh don't know," he groaned. "He wor a grand little chap, wor our Jimmy, and it breaks mi heart to purt wi' him."

"Well, carryin' on like this ull noan bring him back," was the consolatory advise of a mate, "and wi'st aw ha' to dee some day, sooner or later."

For a time the sorrowing father sat with his head buried in his hands. Suddenly he sprang to his feet, and as the tears streamed down his face he cried emphatically: "See yoh, chaps, if it wurn't for th' law Aw'd ha' th' little devil stuffed to look at aw mi life !"

The origin of the phrase, "Worth a guinea a box," applied by the late Mr Beecham to his pills, may not be generally known. Between fifty and sixty years ago, Mr Beecham regularly attended the Ormskirk Market, then, as now, held in the open air, carrying a tray in front of him, on which were his pills, which he sold at 3d a box. One day a boat-woman from Burscough went to him and asked for a box, adding enthusiastically: "Th' last box did me a lot o' good; yohr pills are worth a guinea a box." Mr Beecham instantly seized upon the phrase, cried it with telling effect throughout the day, adopted it as his own motto, and now no term is better known in the advertising world.

Lord Brougham, when plain Mr Henry Brougham, a celebrated pleader, but not equally celebrated for his good looks, was once pleading in the Ormskirk Court, held in the old Town Hall, in those days. He was concerned in a case from the neighbourhood of Burscough, and among the witnesses from that quarter was a boat-woman who used the word "humbug." Brougham pressed her for the meaning of the word. She looked at him straight in the face and said cuttingly: "Well, if Aw were to say yoh were a good-lookin' chap, Aw should be humbuggin' yoh !"

A boat-woman who lived in the Lancashire district was hot in argument upon theology with one of her class when her opponent asked: "Do yoh really believe that a whale swallowed Jonah ?" The reply of the other was emphatic: "Aye! Aw believe my Bible, and —(more emphatic still)— if th' Bible said that Jonah swallowed the whale, Aw'd believe it !"

A good many years ago a woman was committed from Bury on a charge of poisoning her husband. It was alleged that she had put arsenic into his soup for dinner. At the Assizes, she was defended by a well-known barrister, whose forensic ability helped to obtain an acquittal. The accused, on, leaving the dock, in the ecstacy of her gratitude cried out: "God bless you, Mr.—— ! I'll pray for you as long as I live." The barrister did not catch the words, and turning to a turnkey, asked what she had said. On being told slyly: "She may pray for me, but she shall not cook my dinner !"

CHAPTER TEN.

"TIM BOBBIN"—LANCASHIRE PROVERBS—HIGHWAYMEN —THE BURGLARS AND THE VALIANT YEOMAN—HOLDING UP A MAIL COACH.

John Collier, bearing the sobriquet of "Tim Bobbin," by which he was known throughout the length and breadth of the county, was a notable son of Lancashire, born at a house locally known as "Richard o' Jones." He settled at Milnrow, near Rochdale— a place to which in my early days in the Force I made several official visits. There he wrote his "Tummeaus and Meary," in which is enshrined the dialect and humour of the people over one hundred years ago, and there I found that the natives still kept green his memory, never tiring of retailing yarns concerning Tim, which had been handed down to them from their forbears. In his way I learned that his father was a clergyman, and he intended his son also for the Church. But Tim did not seem to take kindly to the paternal plan, and eventually he settled down at Milnrow as the village schoolmaster. He had a keen eye and a ready pen for the humorous, and he was an artist who was reckoned a prodigy among the admiring villagers. he was considered particularly good at landscapes, and his caricatures were vastly entertaining. Tim, moreover, aspired to be something of a dandy, and , indeed, such was his influence that he set the fashion to the young men of the district. An amusing story is told of his power in this respect. One Sunday he had in a joke put on a fancy necklace, and having for a while amused himself and a few choice friends with it he seems to have forgotten the extraordinary ornament, and he actually appeared in church with it. No matter. His admirers thought that what was good enough for Tim was not bad for themselves, and the singular spectacle of young bucks wearing necklaces was witnessed to the no small astonishment and merriment of Tim himself, who had no idea that his joke would have thus developed. an amusing companion, he was welcomed everywhere, and, unfortunately, the love and company led him into habits of intemperance. Tim married a young woman named Mary Clay, who was well educated, having been brought up by a titled lady, and it is probable that she was of great assistance to her husband in his literary compositions. I give the following extract from a letter which Tim Bobbin addressed to a friend, Mr Cowper, a wine merchant, of Liverpool:—

Perhaps your picture you expect
Before I fell the warm effect
Of your car-killing liquor.
But hark you, sir ! The days are dark
And cold; on them I hate aw wark,
As ill as ony vicar.

But in a month or two, at least,
Except the sun wheel back to th' east,
You may expect your beauties.
But in the meantime must I fast ?
Or guzzle ale not to my taste ?
Nay, hang me on some yew trees !

I from my cot, this Christmas eve,
Write with a troubled mind—believe,
And wife in doleful dumps;
For who can merry be, that's wise,
While what he wants is Lerpoo' lies*
And's vexed with jeers and frumps ?

Pray send a line that I may say
To my crooked rib, on such a day,
Your gossip's nose shall job in
A tankard made of mountain wine,
Sweet water, nutmeg, sugar fine,
And set at rest

TIM BOBBIN.
* Liverpool

He remained humorous and facetious to the last. He died in 1786, and was buried in Rochdale Churchyard, the following epitaph, composed by himself, being inscribed upon his tombstone:

"Here lies John, and with him Mary,
Cheek by jowl, they never vary,
No wonder they so well agree—
John wants no punch and Moll no tea."

Lancashire proverbs and sayings are considerable in number, and pithy and to the point in quality, with a touch of characteristic humour. I give a few which I have jotted down:—

"He hangs his fiddle at th' dur sneck." Said of a person who is all life and gaiety with his boon companions, but sullen and sour at home.

"There's mooist thrutchin' wheer there's th' least room."

"It costs a deeal moor playin' than workin'."

"Th' quiet sow eats aw th' draff." Said of one who speaks little, but listens eagerly and uses the information to his own advantage.

"When a chap gets married, he larns what meyl (meal) is a pound."

In choosing a wife, the swain is warned that "fine faces fill no butteries, and fow (ugly) uns rob no cubberts" (cupboards).

We are also told that "an honest mon and a west wind allus goo to bed at neet," "Fleet at meyt, fleet at wark," and "Th' first cock o' hay drives th' cuckoo away."

I give several dialectic words which I have found in any dictionary, but which are in common use in East Lancashire:— "Swailer" (a corn and provender dealer), "swillwood" (firewood), "dilfa" (very bad—in health—evidently from "doleful), "squab" (a sofa, found in Pope's "Imitation of Earl of Dorset," line 10), "neighve" (the fist), and "moo" (a stack of hay or corn inside a building).

In the course of my official life at Ormskirk I picked up many a curious bit of information concerning the "good old days when George III was King," and among them a few facts relative to the desperadoes who were to be found in the district. In 1805 the "Black Bull," between Melling and Aintree, near Liverpool, was kept by a ruffian named Moor, who, with three brothers called Grainger, as accomplices, carried on with success for a considerable length of time a system of highway robbery in the surrounding parts which kept the people in a state of alarm, for those were the days before the establishment of the county police, and detection and apprehension were often slow processes. They were, however, eventually run to earth or dispersed, and most of them executed at Lancaster.

It is related that Dr Wm Bibby, of Ormskirk, made the acquaintance of the highwaymen in a curious manner. He was knocked up one night to attend, so the mounted messenger informed him, "a person in the country." Unsuspicious of anything out of the ordinary, for he was accustomed to calls of this character, he followed his guide, and he was led to a solitary cottage in Melling. Ushered into a back room he found himself in the presence of half-a-dozen men of forbidding appearance, and he betrayed his alarm. "Don't be frightened, doctor," said one, reassuringly, "we shall not hurt you; we only want your professional help." Whereupon a man with a fractured arm was brought to him. Dr Bibby duly attended to him, received his fee, and accepted the invitation to take of refreshments, of which there was no stint. Before he left, however, he was enjoined to secrecy if he valued his life, and having given a promise of secrecy he was dismissed with the information that if at any time he was stopped on the road and he gave his name he would not be molested.

Now it really happened that he was stopped one night on the road near Moor Hall, Aughton, and , remembering the advise, he gave his name and he was allowed to pass on; and only after the gang had been broken up did the doctor divulge his secret.

The above gang in the heyday of its operations seems to have divided itself to carry on different branches of crime, one taking to the highway and another to burglary. About 1810 they broke into the house of Henry Webster, farmer, Melling entering by the kitchen window, under which lay a fierce bitch with her whelps. But she gave no alarm, and I have already pointed out the curious fact proved in cases in which I have been concerned that dogs when fairly cornered in a room from which they have no chance of escape are arrant cowards. The ruffians, having secured a man servant, who slept below, proceeded towards Mr Webster's bedchamber, but he had been awakened by some noise or other, and though without firearms he valiantly disputed their passage at the head of the stairs. There he stood in the dark with an old chair poised in his arms, and as they advanced he felled them one by one. Frantic with rage and pain they fired at him repeatedly, but the darkness was an advantage to him, and their aim was wide. They gave up the struggle in that way and commenced to fire the house, when the plucky farmer was forced to yield. They had learned that he had received a large sum of money two or three days previously, and to force the secret of its hiding place they put halters round the necks of the farmer and his wife, and the ropes were pulled tight over the beams in the ceiling. "Now," said the leader, "give us the money or you hang !" Both protested that there was no money in the house, and the robber, convinced that they were telling the truth, seized what booty they could and decamped.

This outrage led to the farmers and other inhabitants of the district arming themselves and agreeing to take united action if one were attacked, the signal to the rest to be the firing of a gun. For a time the gang escaped. They attempted to "hold up" the mail coach between Aintree and Maghull, but the passengers stoutly defended themselves, and managed to slash the face of one of the thieves with a sword. A number of them soon afterwards, one was found with his face scarred as by a sword cut, and he and the others were executed at Lancaster.

CHAPTER ELEVEN

HORSE BEEF-A MAGHULL MURDERER:
HIS DRAMATIC PROTEST BEFORE THE JUDGE-
A BRUTAL WIFE MURDERER—
A WOMAN'S DOWNFALL AND DREADFUL DEATH—
DRINK THE GREAT CRIMINAL.

Not very long since, this country was profoundly stirred by the revelations respecting the nasty methods under which some of the tinned meat industry of America was carried on. In views of the jeopardy to health and life, reforms were very properly demanded and brought about. That there are wretches in our country, who, though greed of money, are ready enough to put food upon the market full of awful consequences to an innocent public, is unfortunately proved over and over again in one's police experience. Let me give an instance: about fifteen years ago, I had information of a swine fever case in Lydiate, near Ormskirk. In the district were two butchers, who were known as "slink butchers," and between whom there was considerable jealousy. There is an old saying that there is honour among thieves, but I have often found that to be a fallacy. It was so in this case. One worthy informed of the other that he had bought a diseased pig at this particular Lydiate farm. I sent a sergeant and a constable to watch his premises during the night. About three 0'clock in the morning, a butcher's cart from Wigan put in an appearance, but, on catching sight of the police, it was at once driven back again. I, myself, went to the premises, which were just outside the town, accompanied by a veterinary surgeon, medical officer of health, and his assistant, who had been a butcher. We found in an old building the dressed carcases of a pig and calf, both pronounced to be bad, and a carcase of beef, which was declared to be excellent. ! This was most curious, extraordinary - as surprising as a parson chumming with a burglar. Closely questioned on this point, Mr "Slink Butcher" confessed that the beef was horse beef. My friends were staggered and unconvinced, until the man produced the hide buried with the hides of others, in the horse midden. We brought the carcases to Ormskirk and submitted them to a jury of three experienced butchers. They had no difficulty with the pig and the calf, but the beef was pronounced to be of excellent quality, and that of a fine Scotch bullock!

71

CHRONICLES OF A VICTORIAN DETECTIVE

The fact was that the flesh was that of an old worn-out horse which was on its way to the knacker's yard in Liverpool when it was intercepted by the slink butcher, and handed over to him for a guinea. The experts informed of this agreed that the only difference to be distinguished between the dressed carcases of a horse and a cow was that one had a rib more, and that belonged, I believe, to the horse.

The full penalty was inflicted upon the defendant, and his punishment did not end there. He was the licensee of a public-house in the town, and at the next Brewster Sessions I objected to the renewal of the license, with the result that it was taken away.

As the smartest of detectives, hampered with the fallibility which belongs to human nature, cannot always keep with the trail, there are undiscovered criminals. On the other hand, it is singular how frequently a chance word or remark has been the means of bringing men to justice. I will give a couple of instances:-

About 27 years ago a fire was discovered at midnight on the farm premises of Mr John Summer, of Maghull. Sleeping in the blazing building were three or four Irish labourers, among whom was a man known as "Cruise," and he was burned to death. The matter was reported to the coroner by the police-sergeant as having arisen out of an ordinary fire. The night before the inquest was to be held one of these Irishmen called at the police office to inquire whether he would be wanted at the inquest. He was asked what he knew about the fire, and his stolid reply was: "Oi don't know much about it." But the man if he did not know much seemed to be troubled with thoughts - serious and disturbing thoughts; and as he was leaving the office he said simply and with a shake of the head: "Oi think Mullarky done it."

These singular words arrested attention, and on being questioned he observed that Mullarky did not like Cruise, and that he thought he had caused his death. Asked if he knew where Mullarky was, the man said that he had just left him in a beerhouse in Aughton Street, Ormskirk. I sent for him, and when brought into the station I questioned him concerning the fire. He indignantly denied all suggestions, and eventually became insolent. I felt that he knew more than he cared to disclose, and I ordered him to be locked up, and followed this up by sending word to Maghull for every person who knew anything about the affair to be summoned to the inquest.

The Coroner was surprised at my action. Farm fires were of frequent occurrence; he could see nothing out of the common in this one, and he could see no grounds for detaining Mullarky except the suspicions of another Irishman, who appeared to have no grounds for them in fact. But I was not to be shaken in the attitude I had taken up, and the Coroner leaving the examination of the witnesses to me, I gradually drew out circumstances which so told against Mullarky that the jury returned a verdict of murder against him, and the case at the police court, the hearing of which occupied the whole of the day, was further strengthened against him. He was committed for trail, and at the Assizes was defended by Dr. Commins.

The judge, summing up, said that some strong statements had been made in regard to circumstantial evidence such as that upon which that case was built, but he did not agree with them. In his opinion such evidence might carry home conviction to the mind as thoroughly as any other evidence; indeed, in his judgement it was often the most cogent of all evidence,

Prisoner was convicted, and on being asked if had anything to say why sentence of death should not be passed upon him, he said: "Well, sir, I am as innocent of that there crime as the child unborn, if I was never to see the sight of God or Heaven."

Sentence having been passed prisoner said: "Well, sir, you can only judge a fellow on this earth. You cannot judge me in the next, where we shall all be judged. You may not have as much time to pray for your soul as I have. If I were never to see the sight of God or Heaven I am as innocent of the crime which I am going to swing for as the child who is not yet born. I am going before my God now."

The Liverpool Press, in commenting upon the case, expressed the opinion that the public would, in reviewing the evidence, look in vain for any support for Bernard Mullarky's protestation of innocence. Upon these it would be foolish to lay too much stress. Lefroy, the murderer of Mr Gould on the Brighton Railway, and Dr Slade, who poisoned his nephew at Wimbledon, made protests quite as dramatic, and both lived to confess the justice of their doom upon the scaffold. The evidence against Mullarky was certainly circumstantial, but singularly complete.

Mullarky confessed to the murder when in view of the scaffold, and he added: "I have had a short life and a merry one."

The Liverpool Press, again commenting upon the case, questioned whether the annals of crime could disclose such a brutal murder committed on such slight provocation. Continuing, the writer said: "We cannot allow this opportunity to pass without testifying to the decided ability displayed by Mr Superintendent Jervis, of the Ormskirk Police Division, in bringing to light the various phases of this diabolical crime. From the information which was first elicited from eye witnesses it seemed as if the fire on September 25th had been a pure accident, caused presumably by some of the men smoking. Mr Jervis, concluded that there was more in the affair than appeared on the surface, and he at once ordered Mullarky into custody, pending enquiries. The building was examined, and left no doubt as to the origin of the fire. Mr Jervis, with characteristic energy , set to work to complete the chain of evidence he had already begun, and, though he at last succeeded, it was with very great difficulty that he accomplished his object. A complete justification of his suspicions and a striking commentary on his shrewdness are to be found in the result.

As I reflect upon this case and others in which I have been concerned, I am filled with profound wonder at the workings of what we call Providence, Fate, Destiny; and how they move on irresistibly, remorselessly to their end, setting aside the dispositions of man, and often foreshadowing their purpose in a few chance words.

The second case occurred within a few months of the one just related. A collier lived with his wife in a cottage on the outskirts of Skelmersdale. One Friday night - pay day - Turner went home about midnight, more or less the worse for drink. A neighbour both heard and saw him kicking his wife, and this brutality seemed to have been intermittently carried on for several hours. The poor woman died in a day or two afterwards, and her body was found covered in bruises. An Ormskirk doctor, now deceased, was called in to make a post-mortem. Subsequently he came to me at the office, and informed me that there was no necessity to make a thorough post-mortem examination; he had seen sufficient to satisfy him that she "might" have died from natural causes. I said that that would not do; there must be a full and complete post-mortem, and he must make it early next morning with Dr. Dumbreck, of Skelmersdale. He was loth to return to the task, but at any rate he went, and the result was that two doctors were agreed that death had clearly been caused by violence - by kicking. The murder was about as brutal as one could conceive, and the callousness of the man may be gathered from the fact that when he found that his poor wife was dying he suggested to a widow who lived not far away that she should elope with him!

In this case a too ready acceptance of a medical man's first opinions formed on a superficial examination of a victim's body might easily enough have allowed a murderer to escape. Turner, however, was duly convicted on the most ample evidence and was hanged.

The Bickerstaffe murder will be well within the recollection of many readers. In 1901 a collier named Harrison, of no fixed residence, and a woman who was then believed to be his wife, were tramping about the country, and they eventually took an isolated cottage on Bickerstaffe Moss. They had no furniture, and the fact that Harrison entered into possession, by the light of after events, is not without a sinister significance. On the way to the house he was heard to threaten and seen to strike the woman; he was seen to leave it alone; and the same evening he informed the Skelmersdale police that he had that day been to St. Helens, and that on his return he found his wife lying dead on the floor. The inspector, Mr Barnes, acting with intelligence, detained the man and reported the matter to me. A post-mortem was made, proving that the woman had died from strangulation, and that great violence had been used. Here again the evidence, as in most cases of murder, was circumstantial. The prisoner, though denying the crime, told a varying tale of the circumstances of the woman's death . Truth has only one story; the liar changes his as his fears and doubts master him. I had twenty-five witnesses, whose evidence taken together made a damning case against the man. He had met the woman about a year previously, and they were married at Parr Church, near St. Helens. They had led a very irregular life, which culminated for one in that mortal struggle in that lonely cottage. He had strangled her, but she had fought to avoid her fate, and had thrust her hand through the window, cutting her fingers, and thereby in her death throes bequeathing silent but eloquent testimony against her murderer, for there were blood stains upon his wrist bands and other parts of his clothing. The evidence was conclusive; the prisoner was convicted and executed.

There was one curious matter in connection with the case. The doctors who made the post-mortem said that the woman had never borne a child. Yet there was the incontrovertible fact that, twelve years before, she married a respectable tradesman and a property owner living in the northern part of the county, and that she had had three children by him. In those days she was described as an exceedingly handsome woman, but drink was her downfall, and leaving a good home and a good husband she came to that dreadful end, two years after her fight. And her proper name, by order of the Judge, was put upon the indictment in place of that of "Harrison."

A few years ago a murder case at Altcar Camp, in which a Welsh Fusilier was done to death by a comrade, who battered him about the head and left him in a ditch to die, again revealed Drink as the Great Criminal. The two men had been drinking together until the early hours of the morning, then the sudden unreasoning quarrel and the tragedy. It has been the same in all the six murder cases I have had. And reflecting upon the numerous cases which have come under my notice, I see the first false steps which have led to the prison and the scaffold. In many cases it is drink, in others gambling, Sunday driving, mixing with fast companions.

Thirty years ago a gentleman gave me an instance from his own experience of that first wrong step in life. His parents were poor but respectable factory operatives, and he was apprenticed to a tradesman, who had also another apprentice in a youth whose people were in a much social position. One morning when they were sweeping out the shop this second lad found a shilling on the floor, and he pocketed it, with the remark that it did not belong to his master and findings were keepings. My friend - (who was then and is now a Sunday school teacher) - tried to persuade him to mention the matter to the master, but he failed, the finder arguing that as the person who had dropped the coin was not known it was his. He went out to a barber's shop close by and put the shilling on a horse, and that was the beginning of his downfall. He became a gambler, a drunkard, and a thief. My friend, on the other hand, became a partner and ultimately the proprietor of the business in which he had worked as an apprentice. He entered the Town Council, and in a few years he was elected the Mayor of his native town. The first time he took his seat upon the Bench, among the prisoners brought him was the man who had once worked with him as an apprentice. Previous convictions were recorded against him, and the Mayor found it one of the most painful duties of his life in committing that fallen, wretched man to prison.

CHAPTER TWELVE

SLUMS AND THEIR OCCUPIERS - LICENSES AND DRUNKENNESS
- THE EARLY MORNING "NIP" - BEERHOUSE ABOLITION
SUGGESTED - A HINT TO THE TEMPERANCE PARTY.

When I took charge of the Ormskirk Division thirty years ago, I found that ninety per cent of the Ormskirk cases brought before the magistrates were from the courts and alleys of the town. To attack them I knew would raise a hornet's nest about my ears, for the interests in that property were many and strong. I did not hesitate; the right course to me was always stronger than the more popular course, and I began my crusade against this class of property in my annual report to the Bench. Year after year I stuck to my text. More than ten years ago I wrote: "I have before tried to indicate the causes which lead to so much drunkenness in the Division, and i must again, as in previous reports, attribute it (1) to the facilities for obtaining drink, which is out of all proportion to the legitimate requirements of the public......and (2) with regard to Ormskirk, in addition to the excessive number of licensed houses, to the filthy condition of the tenements in most of the courts and alleys. On account of the wretched condition of these dwellings both men and women seem to think it necessary to fly to drink; out of the 211 convictions, 157 were from these places. I will instance Skelmersdale, with a population nearly similar to that of Ormskirk. The number of convictions for drunkenness is 55, whereas in Ormskirk it is 221. Skelmersdale has produced four women drinkers; Ormskirk 54."

Eventually some of the reports were, at the request of the Bench, forwarded to the Local Government Board, with the result that an inspector came down to investigate the whole matter, and his report to the Local Government Board bore out everything I had said in regard to the property. Consequent on this action I had the satisfaction, with many others who had a regard for the public health, of seeing a number of these dwellings demolished. Dwellings, did I say? A great many of them would be better described as hovels and rookeries which were a disgrace to a civilised nation. Most of them were occupied by the Irish population, for whom the owners evidently deemed them good enough. The effect to the cause can surely be traced by the most stupid, in the fact that one of the highest death-rates in the county has been reduced to one of the lowest. And this should be the normal state of Ormskirk's vital statistics. Surrounded by an open country, built upon an elevated site, having an excellent fall for the sewage, and last, but not least, with a capital water supply, the town should be among the healthiest in the Kingdom. As regards to the water forty years ago, when I was in Lancaster an alderman of the borough showed me analyses of different waters in the country, and this is how the first three came out: Glasgow, first; Lancaster, second; and Ormskirk, third.

It struck me as a curious coincidence that during the time I was attacking the slums, and was in turn attacked for that action, I listened to a sermon preached in Westminster Abbey by Cannon J Armitage Robinson, D.D. This was on the 16th July, !899. His text was: "He had compassion on the multitude." The preacher spoke in strong terms—similar to those I had used at Ormskirk, but more eloquently—upon the slums of London and their owners, and I wrote congratulating him upon his action in so doing. He sent me a courteous reply, concluding with: "I have received many letters of sympathy and goodwill since this sermon was preached, but none that I value more than yours."

The sermon, which attracted much attention, was published in extenso, and the Canon sent me a few copies. Upon a subject so important, I take the liberty of making an extract: "Owing to the "landlords' greed for his high rents, tenants are obliged to let off one or "two rooms. . . (typical instances given). . . The consequence "is that tenants are driven into a single room and herded like animals "in a den, without the possibility of living in ordinary decency. . . . "What are our legislators doing ? The laws are stern enough, but the laws "are unavailing unless they can be administered. Through an "insufficiency of houses the landlord is enabled to raise the rent to "a preposterous figure. This may be called 'business'—a name under "which many scandals shelter. But is it a Christian business to grind "the face of the poor ? Are no checks of conscience to be allowed "to limit dividends ? It is unrighteous gained at the cost "of human misery. . . Woe unto you, ye hypocrites ! who devour "windows' houses and for a pretence make long prayers !"

Attacking slums and their owners was not my only unpleasant duty. Ormskirk in those days had perhaps the largest number of licensed houses in the country in proportion to its population. The fully-licensed houses were most of them created in the old coaching days. Stage coaches ceased running sixty years ago, but the beer taps are still running merrily. Beerhouse licenses up to 1869 were granted by the Excise, and there was no difficulty in obtaining one, whilst the magistrates were almost powerless in dealing with them before the Act of 1904. The worst conducted houses were in the neighbourhood of slum property, and were little more than miserable drinking dens, lending an air of truth to the assertion which has become an axiom that slums, drunkenness, and crime are inseparable. How can it be otherwise? Where beerhouses are thick on the ground competition is too keen to permit of a legitimate business. And think of the temptation to the people living under such miserable conditions as I have described, to fly and drink when the facilities were so easy. I am afraid that few of us so circumstanced would have found it easier to have said: "Get thee behind me, Satan !" Much as we may, well housed, well clothed, and well fed, talk pityingly of want of will power and unbalanced minds. The worst evil, however, in my opinion which arises from a close association of drink with family life is that the children are brought up in unhealthy and indecent surroundings. No wonder that they grow up ne'er-do-weels and loafers. Yet not all; flowers spring forth in the most noisome of places, and it has been a pleasure to me to observe within recent years children in their teens and some out of them coming to the police office to ask for a little time in which to pay the fines imposed upon their parents for drunkenness. It has not been uncommon for them to admit all the misery brought to their homes through drinking, and to make the confession that having seen enough of the evils of excessive drinking they had never tasted and never intended to do. This is encouraging even to old police officers who are, perhaps, the greatest of all pessimists, and I believe that in great measure it has been brought about by free and compulsory education. If this be so, the system, expensive as many of us consider it to be, is doing a good which must be of immense importance for the future of this nation. Certain it is that no good examples can be seen or good precepts set in drunken homes with all their miserable surroundings, and that the contrast between them and pleasant school life and the decent world outside must have their influence even upon the young.

To give the children even of the poor a better chance in life it is necessary to reduce the facilities for drink which lie so near many of their homes, and in this direction I have done what I could. In the Lancaster Division I successfully opposed the renewal of several licenses. In the Ormskirk Division, before the Act of 1904, police objection to the renewal of six public-house and 13 beerhouse licenses succeeded, and since 1904 the number has been further reduced by 29.

An evil which has come under my observation in different parts of the county—(and referred to in my annual reports)—is early morning drinking. In my opinion eight o'clock is early enough for men to commence drinking, and it would be to the best interests both of working-men and their families if that hour were fixed instead of six o'clock for the opening of public-houses. Some publicans lay themselves out for an early morning trade. I don't say that they are not within their rights; I merely give it as fact. Their doors are opened exactly at six o'clock—or, perhaps, catching old Father Time by the forelock, a minute or two before. Men on their way to work are tempted to enter, and sometimes it ends in a day's drinking. Scores of working-men's wives had complied to me of this evil, but so far it lies outside the remedy of the police, whose duty is administration, not legislation. Until a later hour is fixed for the opening of licensed houses the evil will continue.

I wonder how many outside the police and those whose business takes them into the poorest quarters of a town realise all that follows from the week-end carouses in the beerhouses adjacent. You enter the miserable houses of these people, and what do you see? Not a piece of furniture to be truthfully called furniture; a couple of old chairs, perhaps, and an orange box; miserable children huddled together on a straw or old matting; their covering a frowsy sack; their father, and as often as not, the mother, drunk; and half the weekly earnings gone in drink. Hundreds of such scenes have I looked upon in Ormskirk and other part of the county.

CHRONICLES OF A VICTORIAN DETECTIVE

The temperance party have excellent arguments on their side, but they are not always used temperately. Licensed houses are necessary, but I would like to see all beerhouses abolished and full licenses given where they are requisite, for the accommodation of man and beast. Licensed victuallers have more at stake than beersellers, and pecuniary interests alone would tend to a better conduct of the houses. They should be in the true sense "Victualling" houses, according to the original intention of the legislature, and a part of them regularly set apart for the supply of refreshments other than intoxicants. By this means the Trade would not only gain in respectability, but many evils which are inseparably bound up with the present system would be swept away.

In 1891, someone, I never heard who, sent copies of my annual report to the magistrates to some of the members of Parliment, and I only learned of this by the receipt of letters from Lord Randolph Churchill, Sir Wm V Harcourt, and Sir Wilfred Lawson. The latter averred that the only way to get rid of the evil was local option. Personally I am not sure that that would work satisfactorily.

Now let me give a case which might have been illustrative of local option. A few years ago a man built a house on the outskirts of the grounds. He applied four or five years in succession for a license, and I successfully opposed the applications. Now, if local option had been in vogue the man was popular with many, and I have no doubt he would have got a license. There are a few villa residences near to that place, and most of the tenants threatened to leave if a license were granted. At one time people in the district were frequently attacked and maltreated, and it was necessary to have two constables patrolling together. Several ruffians were captured and sent into penal servitude for night assaults. Now, with a reduced number of licenses and improvement in slum property the district is becoming respectable.

One of the greatest pleasures I had in connection with licenses was in helping to get rid of an old fully licensed house at Scarth Hill, about a mile out of Ormskirk on the Bickerstaffe road. A great and influential fight was made for its retention, but after a four years' struggle we won. Previous to that we had had numerous cases of drunkenness and assault from that hamlet, but since then, and that is now about sixteen years ago, I don't remember a single case from there. This instance, along with scores of others I could give, shows that where there are unnecessary licensed houses there is an excess of drinking. In the adjoining township, Bickerstaffe, with a population of about 1,100 there is only one inn, yet it ranks as the most sober in the Division, although its people comprise a large number of colliers.

The temperance party in the House of Commons by grasping at too much miss many good things. They made a mistake in rejecting Mr Quilter's Pure Beer Bill, which was introduced some years ago with a regularity which deserved a better fate. If that bill had been passed we should not have had the arsenical beer poisoning cases which occurred a few years ago, while it would have conferred great benefits upon the farming industry.

CHAPTER THIRTEEN

Fifty of sixty years ago the police were strictly confined to patrolling their beats. It was laid down that with them it should be duty first and always, and in their plan of work no provision was made for play. What pleasure they took had to be taken quietly and sadly, or official. foolscap began to be wasted. The promotion of police sports, now so popular, would have been looked upon as a revolutionary step towards the disorganisation of the Force, and the result too often was that thus cut off from reasonable intercourse with the people the attitude of the police towards a community was one of purely stiff and unbending officialism. Yet in those days, or rather a little later, about forty years ago, I came across a case which amusingly illustrates that Lancashire clannishness for all which is "Eaurs" was at times even extended to "Eaur Bobby" when strangers interfered with him. These sturdy beggars called at a rather lonely house in an East Lancashire village, and failing to obtain alms threatened the inmates. The village constable tried to arrest them, and they turned on him. Now a well know character of the place, who had frequently been before the Court for assaults on the police and other persons, at that moment came on the scene. It might have been thought that he would have enjoyed the discomfiture of his official chief enemy. But no. He took off his coat and said: "Aw've helped to thrash a bobby or two misel, but—-Aw'n noan gooin' to see yon devils thrashin' eaur bobby," and he sailed in with his clogs. The fight had scarcely got interesting to the spectators when it was over. Those vagrants from the South were not used to Lancashire clogs, and they went to the lock-ups as meekly as lambs.

Nowadays any decent policeman can rely upon civilian assistance frequently without any call for the same in the King's name, for respectable people have come to realise his necessary position in civilised

84

life, and have experienced in a variety of ways that he is a friend to the community. He is brought more in touch with the public when duty is relaxed, and he can take part in that rational recreation which is required by all men. With a view to promoting a better understanding between the public and the Force in my Division, about 25 years ago I started police sports at Ormskirk, following the example of Manchester, which was, I believe, the first to organise them. I ran them for six of seven years, and their success was such that with the addition of donations from magistrates and a few friends I was able to keep a soup kitchen going for several years after the discontinuance of the sports, whereat in the severity of winter 300 poor children were each night provided with a good hot supper - a great treat to the ragged little urchins who knew not what a "square meal" meant. On several occasions about a hundred of them were supplied with complete suits of clothing, and Paradise was opened to the whole of them on summer excursions to Southport. Further, by the augmentation of the funds as the result of "special efforts" in the shape of concerts, I was enabled to contribute £140 to the Southport Infirmary, £21 to the Southport Convalescent Hospital, £100 to the Ormskirk Cottage Hospital, £120, the cost of a brougham ambulance for Skelmersdale, £100 for the purchase of tools for the miners who lost them all in the Tawd Vale colliery disaster, £15 for the soup kitchen opened at that time in the township, and £150 for investment by the Skelmersdale Urban District Council, the interest of which is annually distributed among the poor widows of miners.

The support given to our various charitable efforts was munificent, affording gratifying testimony to the confidence reposed in the police as almoners, and providing to me that there is a large circle of kind-hearted persons, able and eager to give when they feel that they can rely upon the proper dispensing of their offerings.

Every Christmas Day in Ormskirk 100 hot-pots, each accompanied by a 4lb loaf were given to poor families, together with a number of bed rugs. To the Birkdale Ladies' Association for the Care and Protection of Young Girls and the Society for the Prevention of Cruelty to Animals £20 was subscribed, £100 for prizes for a couple of years or so for the best horses and tableaux in a procession of turnouts, £60 for essays by school children on the subject of kindness to animals, while the innumerable cases in which temporary aid was given are beyond my memory to tabulate.

For all these things I take no credit; we looked upon them as a mere matter of duty which we regarded as something more than the prevention and repression of crime.

A corps in connection with that very useful institution, the St John Ambulance, was inaugurated in Ormskirk about twenty years ago by Mr J. Morison, manager of the Manchester and Liverpool District Bank, and now in retirement at Southport. I was glad to co-operate with him; classes were first held in my office, and afterwards in the Court-room, with the result that nearly every man in the Division succeeded in passing the examinations, and the knowledge and practical skill thus obtained has since proved of great benefit in hundreds of cases. So well has "first aid" been rendered that I am unaware of a single case in which the doctor, called in, has not commended the police for the efficient manner in which they have acted.

One of the first cases occurred at Downholland Bridge. The constable there, being told that the dead body of a man had just been taken from the canal and placed in an outbuilding attached to a public-house, obtained the key, and entering the place at once put into practice the instructions he had received for the resuscitation of the apparently drowned. He continued his efforts for over half an hour, when signs of life appeared, and eventually the man was completely restored and enabled to walk away-one of the most remarkable instances of the snatching of a man out of the very jaws of Death I have ever known. A little knowledge here was not the dangerous thing for which the proverb contends, and in innumerable instances a policeman learns that a little knowledge upon a variety of subjects proves of inestimable value.

I hope that these hints for the apparently drowned may not be deemed out of place:-

Send for medical assistance, blankets and dry clothing. Lay patient flat on his face, folding one arm so that the forehead may rest upon it; put rolled coat, etc., under stomach so as to get the water out; cleanse the mouth and nostrils; draw tongue out with elastic band, unloose tight

CHRONICLES OF A VICTORIAN DETECTIVE

clothing, then try artificial respiration, viz: Place patient on flat surface, body inclined upwards from the feet; support head and shoulders by placing something firm underneath; stand at patient's head, grasp the arms above the elbows, drawing the arms gently and steadily above the head, keeping them there for two seconds, so that air may enter the lungs; then turn down patient's arms, and, pressing them gently and firmly for two seconds against the sides, so as to expel the air from the lungs, persevere continuously until breathing is in the slightest degree perceived. Then, and not before, try all means to promote warmth and circulation, rubbing the limbs and body upwards towards the heart.

N.B—Chief points to be remembered: (1) Never allow patient to be held up by the feet to get water out; (2) send for medical assistance; (3) remove all tight clothing, and dry chest; (4) restore breathing; and (5) promote warmth.

The experiences of the veterans are the finger-posts of the young who would walk the safe and secure path, and in the hope that I may be helpful to young constables I give a few general rules respecting the power of arrest without warrant.

Young constables are naturally at a loss to know their powers of arrest without being armed with a warrant. Now, he can without that instrument apprehend a person who has committed a felony, or if he has reasonable grounds of suspicion that he has committed, or is about to commit, one.

Without a warrant he may deal with lunatics at large, a person doing grievous bodily harm, threatening a life of another, committing arson, breaches of the peace and assaults (if committed in his presence), assaulting or obstructing the police in the execution of their duty, murder, manslaughter, abduction, criminal assault, procuring abortion; guilty of concealment of birth, bigamy, child stealing, robbery, burglary, housebreaking, false pretences, embezzlement, receiving stolen goods; damages to houses, trees, vegetable, and produce generally; killing or maiming cattle, forgery, uttering counterfeit coins; offences under the Prevention of Crimes Act, treason, smuggling, night poaching, desertion from the Army and Navy, peddling without a license, vagrancy, fishing in private waters during the night time, drunk in any highway or public place, and guilty of disorderly conduct; or drunk while in charge of horse, carriage, cattle, or steam engine on any highway or public place; or found on licensed premises during prohibited hours in case of suspicion that the name or address given is false.

CHRONICLES OF A VICTORIAN DETECTIVE

A person who is found so drunk on a highway or public place that he is unable to take care of himself may for safety be arrested and detained until he is sober, when he must be discharged and proceeded against by summons.

A constable may not arrest a person insulting or abusing him by word of mouth, unless he is assaulted or obstructed in the execution of his duty. Where a house requires to be forcibly entered for felony, affray, or breach of the peace, the power should only be enforced where absolutely necessary to guard against the escape of the offender.

No person can be arrested for a mere misdemeanour unattended with violence without a warrant. This rule gives rise to curious instances. A person who is obtained a drove of oxen of a flock of sheep by false pretences, and is not "found committing" the offence within the meaning of the Larceny Act of 1861, may go quietly on his way, and no one, not even a police officer, can apprehend him without a warrant. But a man offers to sell any person a piece of dead fence, supposed to have been stolen, he may be apprehended by that person and required to show that he came lawfully by it. To entitle a person to the protection of the Larceny Act 1861, and other similar statutes, the arrest must be immediate, and he must have acted under a bona-fide belief in the guilt of the party. It would be a question for the jury in an action for malicious prosecution whether the arrest was "immediate."

A private person may apprehend, without a warrant, on view of a breach of the peace, and before the affray is over, and deliver the offender over to a constable, if there are reasonable grounds for believing in its continuance or immediate renewal.

The general rule is that "For the sake of the preservation of the peace, any individual who sees it broken may restrain the liberty of him whom he sees breaking it so long as his conduct shows that the public peace is likely to be endangered by his acts; but if a man without authority attempt to arrest another illegally, it is a breach of the peace, and any other person may lawfully interfere to prevent it, doing no more harm than is necessary for that purpose."

CHRONICLES OF A VICTORIAN DETECTIVE

A police-constable cannot arrest without a warrant on a charge of misdemeanour. A person apprehended without a warrant must be taken before the magistrates as soon as practicable, and if it be not practicable within 24 hours he ought to be bailed by recognisances, unless the offence is a serious one. But whether the apprehension was with or without warrant there should be no unnecessary or unreasonable delay in taking the person before a justice.

A magistrate enjoys the same latitude as a constable of arresting a person on reasonable suspicion of having committed a felony—without being called upon to prove that the felony has actually been committed. But he cannot arrest a person who is guilty before his eyes of a misdemeanour, where there is not a breach of the peace and where there is no necessity to arrest the offender to prevent a renewal of the act.

Imprisonment under a warrant of commitment runs from the date on which the prisoner is received by the governor of the prison. Consequently a person arrested on Saturday and not taken to prison until Monday would be kept in custody two days longer than the time specified in the warrant. The prisoner, therefore, should be conveyed to gaol with all possible despatch, or the constable executing the warrant might have some difficulty in defending an action for false imprisonment.

It has been held that a constable has no right to handcuff a person whom he has attempted to escape, or it is necessary to prevent him from escaping.

The following are some of the rules of evidence established by decisions of the Supreme Court:- A person is presumed to be innocent until the contrary is proved. Leading questions must not be put to witness, that is, questions so framed as to suggest the answer described. For instance: "Did you see the prisoner at 8-30 on the night of the 19th inst. in Short street talking to the deceased ?" That is a gross leading question which in itself suggests the answer. The witness must himself state the circumstance under which he met the prisoner. Hearsay evidence is not admissible. The statement of one prisoner is not evidence against another. Conversations taking place out of the hearing of the party effected cannot be given in evidence. Evidence of an accomplice is admissible, but is not reliable except it be corroborated by some collateral proof.

Evidence obtained from a prisoner influenced by any threat, promise, or inducement held out to him by any person concerned in the prosecution is inadmissible. A servant girl was asked by the mother of the child found dead in a ditch whether she had had anything to do with its disappearance, where upon the girl weepingly said: "If you won't send for the police I will tell the the truth." The mistress replied: "I will not hurt you, but if you tell the truth you will be much happier." The prisoner then confessed to having caused the child's death, but at the Assizes that evidence was deemed inadmissible. In a murder case at the Somerset Assizes in 1877 a superintendent of police stated that in a conversation he had with the prisoner asked him if he could account for himself on the Thursday night. The Lord Chief Justice told the superintendent that the law did not allow a man under suspicion and about to be apprehended to be interrogated at all.

Certainly, it is the duty of the police to make enquiries of any person likely to throw any light upon the circumstances of a crime, but when an officer intends to arrest a person questions are not to be put to him; he must simply be told the nature of the offence for he is arrested, and the officer should keep his ears and eyes open. Any statement then made by the prisoner is evidence, and should be carefully noted down for future production.

There are three matters which I have always strongly impressed upon the men joining my Division. Firstly, that truthfulness under all circumstances should be strictly adhered to, for it is cowardly to lie, and only cowards are liars. Secondly, that sobriety is essential to the constable if he would do his duty; and thirdly, that civility should be shown to all classes of the population. The police should not be too fond of showing their authority, and they should never forget that the Force was established for the protection and not the oppression of the public and that there duty should be directed to (1) the prevention of crime, (2) the detection of offenders, and (3) the preservation of the peace.

CHAPTER FOURTEEN

THE POLICE CONSTABLE ANCIENT AND MODERN
- THE KINGDOM'S POLICE FORCE - SUGGESTED REFORM -
THE LANDLADY AND HER BROTHER-IN-LAW.

The reader may be disposed good humouredly to smile at the title have given to this chapter as one comprising historical facts which must be outside one's reminiscences. True, they are, but historical matters as they may be they have for me an interest pardonable, perhaps, in one who has spent fifty-seven years in connection with the Lancashire County Constabulary, and I hope they will be found of some interest to the general reader.

The office of constable is a very old one, for, according to the common law of our ancestors, every freeman was a pledged constable or conservator of the King's peace. He was answerable to the principal residents of his district for the good conduct of himself and his neighbours, the headmen were answerable to the chief officers of the shires, and they were responsible to the Earls.

Parlimentary legislation commenced in the 12th century. In the year 1166, by the Assize of Clarendon, the Saxon system of frank-pledge, or mutual security for the preservation of the peace, was re-established; and visiting justices were commissioned to receive the recognizances and to administer justice.

In 1181, by the Assize of Arms, the duty was cast upon every freeman of bearing arms for a purpose of enforcing the preservation of the peace and of pursuing and overcoming criminals. If any suspected traveller, any stranger for whom no person had given pledge, or any malefactor was discovered in any district, it was the duty of the inhabitants to arrest him, and if he fled it was the duty of the principal inhabitant (the headborough) to raise the hue and cry. Every adult in the neighbourhood immediately on hearing the cry was bound to follow the chase with his household, and all the men of his land with such arms as each was entitled to bear for this purpose, and to track the fugitive through their own land to the furthest limits, where they were again to raise the headboroughs and freemen of the adjoining land to take up the hue and cry, and to pass it from domain to domain until the criminal should be caught.

By the Statute of Winchester (1285) the gates of all walled towns were to be shut from sunset to dawn, and at each gate a watch was to be set to arrest all strangers and suspected travellers. These were perhaps the earliest organisations of the two classes of police, town and rural - a distinction which is continued by the modern system of county and borough police. In process of time citizens gradually evaded the elementary duties of citizenship by paying deputies to do their policing for them. Then the paid constable was enrolled, of whom Shakespeare presents us with delightful samples in Dogberry and Verges, who never wilfully ran into danger, and who, in the words of one of their men, "would rather sleep than talk, and who knew what belonged to a watch!" The which honest Dogberry commends in these words: "Why you speak like an ancient and most quiet watchman; for I cannot see how sleeping should offend: only have a care that your bills be not stolen!"

In the seventeenth century the regular pledging of citizens to constabulary duties at Court Leets having fallen into desuetude it was provided by a Statute that "as Lords of Manors do not keep annual Court Leets regularly, in case any constable, headborough, or tighingman go out of the parish, or die, two justices may make and swear a new one until the next Court Leet, or until the next Quarter Sessions of the Justices; and after a year's services may be discharged by Justices at Quarter Sessions, and successors appointed by them until the next Court Leet." Eventually the function of the Court Leet as to the appointment of constables lapsed, and was cast upon the Justices of the Peace. In the year 1842 was passed the Parish Constables' Act, which provide that no peace officer under any name of office should be appointed for any parish, township, or village, except for the performance of duties unconnected with the preservation of the peace of any Court Leet. By the same Act it was enacted that henceforth parish constables to be employed as peace officers should be appointed by Justices in Petty Sessions once a year. By the more recent Act, 1872, such constables are now to be appointed whenever the Court of

CHRONICLES OF A VICTORIAN DETECTIVE

General or Quarter Sessions of the County shall deem it necessary with the view to the preservation of the peace and they are to be subject to the authority of the Chief Constable of the County.

By the Watching and Lighting Act of 1833, previsions was made for the watching of every parish and town by a committee of the ratepayers, and thus one sees the rise of Watch Committees which in our boroughs have the control of the Police Force in their hands, and are responsible for the good government of the town.

The final establishment of the modern system of County and Borough Police Forces was enacted under the Act of 2 and 3, Vic C 93 (Sir Robert Peel's Act—hence police are sometimes called "Bobbies" or "Peelers"), and 3 Vic C 88, and subsequent Acts. These Acts provide for the establishment of a Constabulary Force for the whole of every county, under one Chief Constable. This Act 2 and 3 Vic was permissive. Lancashire was the first county to take advantage of the permission, and in 1839 established its own forces (in 1856 the Act became compulsory). The county commenced with a force of 500, a year or two later it was reduced to 350, but almost immediately was again raised to its original strength. Its stood at those figures when I entered the service nearly fifty-eight years ago, and that number policed the whole county, with the exception of Liverpool and Manchester, and two or three old borough towns. On the same ground covered by that small force is now a force numbering about 3,000; this shows the rapid growth of the county.

The Police Force of Great Britain and Ireland number about 60,000 which will average one constable to about every 670 of the inhabitants. The strength of the London Metropolitan Force is 15,694, or one constable to about every 414 of the inhabitants. City of London strength is 928 (this does not include 298 on duty at the London and India Docks, and 50 at the Central Meat Market), or one constable to every 40 of the inhabitants. The acreage is small, 668, but then in this area there is no town or city in the world where such vast wealth can be found in so small a space. The valuation amounts to £4,424,609. The following may be cited in comparison:- Liverpool: Acreage, upwards of 15,000; valuation, £3,910,369. Manchester: Acreage, 12,911; valuation, £2,955,775. If, say, one-half of this force were trained to the use of the rifle-in case this country should ever be threatened by an invasion - 30,000 strong, active, and well-trained men would form a valuable safeguard to our shores.

The cost of the police in the United Kingdom is about £5,350,000, the cost per man about £96, or about 2s 9d per head of the population, one-half of which is provided by the Imperial Exchequer. The London Metropolitan, the Royal Irish Constabulary, and the Dublin Police are under the Government; and the counties are under Standing Joint Committees of the County Councils, which are composed of County Justices and members of County Councils. those cities and boroughs having their own police are under the control of the Town Councils.

I have often been asked if I could suggest any scheme for the improvement of the Police Force. I admit that at present the system is established on a good basis, but it is not perfect. The division of concurrent areas among several independent forces leads too often to confusion, unavoidable delay, and unnecessary expense, and, in spite of everything, jealousy and rivalry frequently exist, not only between neighbouring forces, but also between departments in the same service. I am satisfied that greater efficiency and economy would be promoted by unification on lines similar to those laid down in Lord Cross's Measure dealing with the prisons. The police would then be able to do their duty more independently than they can at present, especially in small areas. As an Imperial force they would not be subjected to the tyranny of local prejudices, and the petty control of the Little Minds; they would have to seek the favour of no class, and they would be able to do their duty fearlessly without any thought of favour on the one hand or fear of consequences on the other.

One instance will show how police in small boroughs are handicapped. I had charge of the Lancaster County Division. In addition to my other duties I was Inspector of Weights and Measures for the Borough of Lancaster. On visiting the public houses on one occasion to examine their measures I found at one place half-a-dozen tall ale glasses a little short of measure. They were rather expensive glasses and I did not like the idea of seizing them, so I suggested to the landlady that if she would remove them from the bar, and not use them in the course of trade, I would not take them. She asked what I meant by "taking" them. I explained to her that if I took them I should have to summon her. Her indignant retort was: "I like that! I'd soon be at my brother-in-law's - he's a member of the Town Council." Upon that I told my assistant to take charge of the glasses, and to the landlady I said: "I am going to take them and summon you, and you can tell your brother-in-law that I care as much for him and the Town Council as I do for you." A rather penalty was inflicted.

In England and Wales there are three Inspectors-General, whose duty it is to report annually to the Home Secretary as to the efficiency or otherwise of the forces within their jurisdiction, and on their report the Imperial grant is made or rejected, as the case may be. In counties there is required at least one constable to every 1,000 of the inhabitants. But then the counties have this advantage, in case of tumults or demonstrations of any kind in any part of the county, detachments from other parts of the county are at once sent to those districts.

CHAPTER FIFTEEN

PRISONERS, ANCIENT AND MODERN—
THE JEWISH SAMSON GRINDING CORN—APOSTLE PAUL'S PRISON
—JOHN HOWARD, THE PHILANTHROPIST—PRISON REFORMS.

Having given a brief history of the origin and development of the police-constable, a short account of prisons may not be without interest. The earliest record of a prison, so far as my researches go, is that in Genesis, where it is written that Joseph was imprisoned under false accusation of Potiphar's wife. This was probably 2,000 B.C, and his period of imprisonment—light no doubt in his case because he "found favour in the sight of the keeper of the prison"— extended over at least two years.

To the Jewish prisons there are frequent allusions in the Scriptures; they seemed to have consisted of one part where there was mere confinement, of "inner prisons," darker and more wretched, and of dungeons where death itself put a happy period to the sufferings of the victims. Attached to the prisons seem to have been courts wherein prisoners were allowed to transact business, while to the fact that Samson, imprisoned, "did grind corn in the prison house," goes to prove that among the Philistines whose territories bordered on those of the Israelites the labour of the prisoners was sometimes turned to good account.

Horrible tortures were practised by the Persians, Phoenicians, Egyptians, and Carthaginians; with them cruelty was a studied science; for centuries it formed the principal part of prison treatment, yet probably for diabolical ingenuity in torture the ancients never approached the Spanish Inquisitors, who, under the cloak of religion, dealt with their victims by fiendish methods which have been unparalleled.

In ancient Rome the first prison was built by Ancus Marcius, the forth king of that city, and the second erected by Servius Tullius, the sixth king, was known as the Tullianum, and was a State prison with dungeons. The Apostle Paul was said to have been imprisoned for a second time in the dungeon of the Mamertine prison. In this and others early Christians were tortured and cruelly done to death. The state of society is shown by the

96

building of additional prisons, the necessity for which Juvenal in his third satire thus bewails:— "Happy ancestors ! Fortunate ages ! which of yore under kings and tribunes saw Rome satisfied with a single prison."

The dark ages of prison life extended from the earliest times to the beginning of the 18th century. Yet some attempt at reform had previously been made in England in the reign of Edward VI. In 1550 Latimer spoke out strongly against the condition of the London prisons, and recommended the appointment of paid chaplains, remarking: "It is a holy day work to visit the prisoners." But all efforts at reform seemed to have been feeble and spasmodical, though we find with a view to the betterment of the condition of prisoners that towards the close of the 16th century, in Elizabeth's time, Bernard Gilpin visited the gaols of the northern counties.

It was not until after the formation of the Christian Knowledge Society at the end of the 17th century that any real attempt at reform was made. Then committees were formed to inspect Newgate and the Marshalsea, and to report to that institution. Their report presents a sad picture of the abuses and immoralities of those gaols. Among the suggestions made for their improvement were that prisoners should be separately confined and that a regular plan should be laid down for their moral and mental improvement. The society itself, with this end in view, sent books to every prison in England.

Pope Clement XI., one of the most enlightened of the Pontiffs as well as an active prison reformer, in 1704 established the juvenile prison of St Michael's for boys and youths on the plan of discipline now known as the "Auburn system." Howard the great philanthropist, visited this place, and was warm in his condemnations. Over the portals he found this inscription: "Clement XI reared this prison for the reformation and education of criminal youths to the end that those when idle had been injurious to the State might, when better instructed and trained, become useful to it. In the year of grace, 1704, of the Pontiff, the forth." Within, upon a marble slab let into the wall, was this sentence: "It is of little use to restrain criminals by punishment unless you reform them by education."

This is now acknowledged as the true policy in prison reform, but it was then all the more remarkable as the expression of an enlightened mind, and amid all the horrors of torture which surrounded prison life in every country; and so it was that the example of one advanced reformer was only very slowly copied by others.

It took over 200 years to pass Latimer's recommendation of paid chaplains into law. But there was rising a man who with a voice of thunder was to catch the ears of the people on the subject. In 1773 John Howard was, at the age of forty six, appointed High Sheriff of Bedfordshire. He actively discharged the duties of that position; he visited the prisons of the county; the sufferings the miseries, and injustices he saw filled him with indignation, and by word and deed he set to work to remedy the evil. He was not satisfied to remain in his own county. He went through England, Scotland, and Ireland, and crossed to the Continent. Everywhere he found cruelty, loathsomeness, dirt, and disease; and the result of his experiences was published in 1777. Both in England and on the Continent the book made a great sensation. Subsequently Howard penetrated even to Russia in his investigation of prison life; and it was while on this holy mission that he sacrificed his life. At Cherson, on the Black Sea, he was sent for to see a lady who was suffering from an infectious disease, so greatly had his fame as a doctor to prisoners spread. At first he declined the invitation, on the plea at he only visited the poor. But at length he yielded importunity, and went and prescribed for the lady. She grew worse, and he was again called to attend her. He obeyed the summons upon a bitterly cold and wet day; his journey chilled him to the bone, yet he attended his patient, but it was at the cost of his life; he caught the fatal disease, and in the course of a week passed away at Cherson.

In life Howard had forced on great improvements, and prisons from dens of wickedness and vice were gradually being converted into places where there was hope for the criminal. But for some time after his death the work languished, and it was not until a quarter of a century had elapsed before it was resumed by Mrs Elizabeth Fry, William Allen, Stephen Gellet (the American Quaker), and others. Mrs Fry was a power among the Quakers by reason of her aristocratic connections, her own personal goodness, and her husband's wealth, and she accomplished a great deals of good. With only one lady companion she visited Newgate, distributing clothing among the women and holding religious services. A school was also established for the instruction of the women, and "An Association for the Improvement of Female Prisoners in Newgate" was formed. The inmates were also encouraged to work, and the produce of their labours was sold. Other philanthropists, among them Wilberforce, took up the work, and eventually Mr Secretary Peel, afterward Sir Robert Peel, passed his well-known Gaol Act of 1823. It was also Sir Robert Peel who passed the Police Act of 1839. Under the Act of 1823 female prisoners were placed in the charge of female officers, short daily services were held in the chapel, reading and writing taught, the gaoler's power curtailed, and quarterly reports submitted to the Court of Quarter Sessions, with the consequences that the prisons were reorganised and discipline improved.

The Reformatory system may be traced to the indefatigable services of Howard. He wrote and toiled to establish a method of treatment for young delinquent children, where the perils of bad surroundings might be averted, and criminal proclivities eradicated, with a view to their being saved for an honest and industrious life. "Boys," he said, "confined for correction should be separated from other prisoners, and, indeed, from one another. A kind and tender monitor should often see them, and, without tiring their attention, converse with them as a friend and parent."

The necessity for this reformation was shown in a report made in the early part of the 19th century, in which it was stated that crimes of the worst description were committed by boys, that 8,000 in the Metropolis gained their living by thieving, and that a large proportion were constantly passing through the prisons and so becoming hardened criminals. The chief causes were found to be homelessness, parental neglect, want of mental, moral, and religious education, the corrupting influences of prison, drink, debauchery, and all kinds of wickedness.

In 1830 the Children's Friendly Society opened a small industrial school at Hackney Wick, for boy vagrants. Subsequently Miss Murray, maid of honour to Queen Victoria, joined the enterprise, and not long after her accession the Queen herself established at Chiswick a girl's school on similar lines, calling it the "Victoria Asylum," and this was the first institution to which her Majesty gave her name and support. In the second year of reign (1839) was passed the first Act dealing with the work of juvenile reformation.

In 1854 the Youthful Offenders' Act was passed, and its amendment of 1855, 1856, and 1857 were consolidated in 1866. The Act was the outcome of meetings held in Birmingham, led by Mr Commissioner Hill, its then Recorder, and the success of its operations has been such that an American writer said of it: "That magnificent system of reformatory and industrial schools, which in my opinion make England the leader and model of the world in this truly God-like work."

Private philanthropy in many places has munificently augmented State effort in reformatory work, while in recent years the legislature by various Acts have shown an increasing earnestness to check incipient criminality in the young and to work on lines which are the best calculated to bring about a real and abiding reformation of conduct.

CHAPTER SIXTEEN

ONE HUNDRED YEARS AGO—LANCASTER CASTLE RECORDS
—DEATH PENALTIES FOR THEFT—BURGLARY AND FORGERY—
A SOLICITOR'S ACTION—A SHORT WAY WITH REFORMERS

Inspired by the late Mr Justice Hawkins, who wound up his "reminiscences" which extract from the Newgate Calendar, I offer some passages from the Lancaster Castle Records for the contemplation of those who yet sigh for the "good old days when George was King."

September 12, 1801.—Eight men executed, viz., Thos Walmsley and Arthur Garaghty, for uttering forged notes; William Gallant, for endeavouring to seduce a soldier from his duty; Isaac Slater, for stealing printed calico; John Rhodes, for highway robbery; and Joseph, John, and Simon Mason, brothers, for burglary.

April 13, 1802—John Nutcher, for mail robbery, and Patrick McConville, for uttering a forged note, were hanged.

September 2, 1802—Henry Hurst, for the murder of John Kay at Bury, was executed.

The reader will now begin to understand the origin of the saying, "One might as well be hanged for a sheep as a lamb." One might as well break the whole Decalogue as stop at one offence when the punishment was the same.

September 18, 1802—Elias Gibson, for forming a will, and Nicholas Sherlock, for highway robbery, executed.

February 21, 1803—Thirteen persons were tried for high treason. Colonel Despard and eight others were found guilty and executed in the presence of 20,000 persons. Lord Nelson gave evidence for the gallant officer, but nothing could save him in the days when George III was king, and fear and not justice ruled the minds of rulers.

CHRONICLES OF A VICTORIAN DETECTIVE

March 13, 1803—Thirty prisoners for trial. Of the number eleven were condemned to death and five were executed; Patrick Quigley, Henry Rice, and Thomas Ward, for burglary at Wavertree; Wm. Elsworth, for similar offence at Burnley; and George Short, for sheep stealing. Two persons were convicted of manslaughter and sentenced to be burnt in the hand and one year's imprisonment. Criminals were burned in the hand with "F" for "felon."

April 11, 1804—Two men—Barker and Chadwick, for burglary at Oakenclough—executed.

May 5, 1804— Joseph Brown, for highway robbery, executed.

September 8, 1804.—John Ogilvey and Thomas Smith, for forgery; Thomas Boadle, James Bridge, and John Bradshaw Magee, for uttering forged notes, were executed.

March, 1805—John Lever, for murder; James Richardson and Thos. Conley, for forgery; Charles Berry, for burglary; William Davis, for stealing £57; and Robert Riley, for stealing two cows, were all hanged.

April, 1806—Mary Jackson, for felony; James Foxcroft, for burglary; and Chris Simpson, for highway robbery, were executed.

April, 1808.—Mary Charnley, aged 19, for robbing her master's house in Liverpool, was hanged.

April, 1809.—Seven men executed.

August, 1809—Nine prisoners sentenced to death for highway robbery robbery, felony, and uttering forged notes.

September, 1811.—Five men, for robbery and burglary, executed.

May, 1812.—A special commission was opened at Lancaster for the trial of rioters before the Hon. Baron Thompson and the Hon. Sir Simon le Blane. Eight prisoners, viz., James Smith, Thomas Kerfoot, Job Fletcher,

CHRONICLES OF A VICTORIAN DETECTIVE

Abraham Charlson, John Howarth, John Lee, Thomas Hoyle, and Hannah Smith, were hanged on the 16th June following. A troop of Blues attended the execution, and four companies of the Berkshire Militia were also under arms.

March, 1812, and March 1813—Six men at each of these Assizes were left for execution. In the following years the number rose to thirteen, and the March Assizes, 1815, John Warburton, for highway robbery; Moses Owen, alias Lodge, for horse stealing, were sentenced to death; James Duncan, Benj. Duckworth, Wm Orrell, John Smith, and James Hulme, for stealing bank notes from the person of Wm. Ellison at Garstang, were transported for life.

May, 1816—Jones, alias Leonard, for forgery, executed.

August, 1816.—No less than 31 persons were sentenced to death, but 24 of the sentences were commuted to transportation for life. Executed: Susannah Holland, for the murder of her husband—her body given to the doctors for dissection; John Jones, John James, Michael Maguire, and James Barrow, for burglary; and James McLean Boyd, for selling forged notes.

At the March Assizes, 1817, and the August Assizes of the same year, ten and eleven prisoners were respectively left for execution, two being women, for uttering forged notes.

At the latter Assizes, before Chief Baron Richards and Baron Wood, a most extraordinary action was heard, in which Mr Hodgson, a solicitor, of Whitehaven, sued Mr Scarlett, barrister (afterwards Lord Abinger), for defamation. Plaintiff pleaded that ha had been injured in his character by certain slanderous words spoken of, and concerning, him by the defendant in open Court at the last Assizes for Lancaster. Mr Raine and Mr Richardson appeared for the plaintiff, and Mr Topping, Mr Sergt. Hullock, and Mr Littledale for the defendant Mr Hodgson was the attorney for the plaintiff in a case tried at Lancaster, in which Mr Scarlett was the counsel for the defendant, and in the course of his speech he used the following words, the subject of complaint: "Sometimes actions are founded in folly;

some actions are founded in knavery; some actions arise out of the folly, and some out of the knavery of the attorney; some in the folly of the parties, and others in their knavery. The attorney for the plaintiff drew this promissory note, and fraudulently got Beaumont to advance £150, which was a most profligate transaction on the part of Mr Hodgson;" and then he proceeded to make the district allegation: "Mr Hodgson is a wicked and fraudulent attorney."

His Lordship said that although the words used might be too severe he was of opinion that the action could not be maintained. The plaintiff was therefore non-suited.

August 28th, 1819—Henry Hunt and others calling themselves "Radical reformers," who demanded among other things "annual Parliaments, universal suffrage, and election by ballot," were brought to Lancaster Castle on a charge of high treason, afterwards reduced to conspiracy. This was a sequel to a meeting held at Manchester dispersed by the Yeomanry, who killed four persons and wounded about 400, which, happening on St Peter's Fields, was afterwards known as "Peterloo." Hunt and his friend were bailed out, but though the grand jury at Lancaster returned true bills they declined at those Assizes to take their trial. In the following year Hunt, who had got his trial removed to York, was with his companions found guilty "of assembling with unlawful banners, an unlawful assembly for the purpose of moving and inciting the liege subject of our Sovereign Lord, the King, into hatred and contempt of the government and constitution of the realm as by law established, and attending the same." Hunt was sentenced to be imprisoned for two years and six months, and find sureties for his good behaviour during a further term of five years. Several of his companions were sentenced to a year's imprisonment.

March Assizes, 1920. - Thirty four prisoners were capitally convicted, and out of them six were left for execution: J. Dun, for murder; John Todd, Philip Rogers and Peter McCormick, for uttering forged notes; and Wm. Parker and Charles Miller, for highway robbery.

August Assizes in the same year - Thirty two prisoners were capitally convicted, but only two were left for execution, viz., Wm. Hall for highway robbery, and Hy. Houghton for forgery.

Two lads, John Wilson (18) and John Johnson (17), for stealing from the shops of Robert Knight and Thos. Calvert, of Lancaster, were transported for life; and John Spencer, for stealing a gelding, was sentenced to death.

Under date May, 1821, is recorded a curious incident. A mare with a man asleep on her back walked up to the stable door of Mr Salthouse, of Scotforth, and was recognised as one which had been stolen from him two years previously. It is not stated whether the man was taken or whether the owner was so overjoyed at the recovery of the property that he allowed the rider to escape. It is certainly a singular instance of memory on the part of that animal.

June 1st, 1822. - The body of Major Gerrard, who was drowned while on a fishing excursion near Southport on May 30th, was washed up at Cockerham Sands.

August 21st, 1826. - Alexander and Michael McKean, brothers, were executed for murder, and their bodies given to the doctors for dissection. So on March 22nd, 1828, Jane Scott, for the murder of her mother, was handed and her body given to the surgeon. We have noticed how forgery was capitally dealt with, but at the March Assizes, 1829, we find that John Williams, an attorney, was among the lucky ones. Sentenced to death for that crime he was respited - for what reason does not transpire.

Upon some of the banners used on the occasion which led to the trial of Hunt and some of his companions were inscribed: "No Corn Laws," "Universal Suffrage," "Vote by Ballot," "Annual Parliaments," "Union is Strength," "Unite and be Free," "Taxation without Representation is Unjust and Tyrannical," "Let us Die like Men and Not be Sold like Slaves," and " Equal Representation or Death."

CHAPTER SEVENTEEN

A PLAN TO ESCAPE FROM LANCASTER CASTLE - A SCOUNDREL'S FALSE CHARGE - THE "GOOD" OLD HANGING DAYS- A CONVICT'S SUCCESS.

At the Lancaster Assizes, held on the 21st of March, 1818, Chief Baron Richards presiding in the Crown Court, there were 128 prisoners for trial, and of these no less than 49 were sentenced to death. These Assizes were made noteworthy by an organised attempt of the prisoners, on receiving their sentences, to escape from the Castle. Their plans had been well laid and nearly executed when the plot was discovered.

It is worthy of remark that at this period the law did not allow the sun to set a second time upon a murderer after he was convicted, unless a Sunday intervened. Hence it was usual for the judges to try such cases on the Friday in order that the criminal might have the longest time allowed by the law. The execution of murderers generally took place at 8 o' clock on Monday morning. The hour yet remains, but all publicity in connection with the executions has long been abolished.

I have previously maintained, by examples, that circumstantial evidence, if of course complete, is far more satisfactory than direct evidence, because there is always the danger that the latter may be manufactured to procure the ruin of a person, while in the marshalling of the circumstances of a crime there is often a silent yet convincing evidence which no words can controvert. Let me give a case in point. In the "Lancaster Gazette", dated February 28th, 1830, I find the following paragraph: - "Mr Robert Stanley, of Oswestry, was attacked about a mile from this town by two men, one of whom knocked him down with a bludgeon, the blows rendering him insensible, and while in that condition he was robbed. When he recovered he found himself fastened to a gate by strong wire tied round his hands and neck. Two men and a woman were apprehended upon suspicion, and committed for trial at the Assizes."

CHRONICLES OF A VICTORIAN DETECTIVE

Here is the record at the March Assizes, 1830: - Paul Rigby, John Grimes, and Mary Grimes, charged with the highway robbery of Robert Stanley, of Scotforth, on the 23rd February, were found guilty and sentenced to death.

A later edition of the "Gazette" gives an account of the miraculous escape of these prisoners from an ignominious. It transpired that no such person as Robert Stanley, a joiner, had ever lived at Oswestry as represented by the prosecutor; and that the whole story of the robbery was a trumped up one, in order to raise subscriptions on his behalf. Evidence was forthcoming that a person exactly answering the description of the man calling himself Stanley had in several other places succeeded in having subscriptions raised for himself by a similar artifice. In this case the scoundrel decamped before he could be apprehended. The prisoners were discharged from custody.

Capital punishment, for what are now considered trifling offences was enforced until 1832. It was thought that the best mode of advancing civilisation and improving the morals of the people was to hang from ten to twenty persons every Monday morning at the Old Bailey, and a proportionate number in the provinces, and that for offences which are now expiated by fines and short terms of imprisonment.

At the Lancaster March Assizes in 1832 Baron Parke stated that two Acts had been recently passed; one abrogating the punishment of death in all cases connected with the counterfeiting of the current coin of the realm; the other Act abolishing the death penalty in all cases of cattle stealing or stealing to the value of £5 from a dwelling house, but making the punishment in all cases transportation for life.

Punishment of death for forgery remained on the Statute Book until the accession of Queen Victoria in 1837, and hanging in chains, though it had fallen largely in desuetude was not actually abolished until 1832. Horse stealing, sheep stealing, burglary, and house breaking were all, until the year 1830, punishable by death.

CHRONICLES OF A VICTORIAN DETECTIVE

Under the more humane dispensation of this age brutal punishments have passed away, and there is still a steady movement forward for the reclamation of the criminal as well as his punishment. There may be little hope for the aged criminal as for the aged pauper, but as with pauper children, so with the young criminally inclined, a bright light shines across their pathway leading to reformation. Statistics of work done give encouragement for the future, and as poverty and misery, the parents of crime, disappear, so may we hope to see the dawn of the era of real Christianity in the Kingdom.

I have often wondered what became of those whom I was instrumental in sending to Botany Bay, but in only one case did I learn anything of his subsequent career. Very early in my service - in 1850 or 1851 - I had a young man at the Preston Quarter Sessions for felony. It was his third offence, and in those days, however trifling the felonies, a third conviction meant transportation. This man was sentenced to seven or ten years, I cannot now remember which. About the year 1877 I heard that shortly after landing at Botany Bay he managed to escape, made his way up the country, obtained work at a blacksmith's shop and was doing well, when he was discovered and arrested. After a little while he was liberated, and, commencing business on his own account, he became very successful, and died about 1875, leaving upwards of £12,000.

My self-imposed task is finished. Out of my fifty seven years official connection with the Lancashire County Constabulary I have drawn experiences which I thought might be instructive as well as entertaining to the reader. I entered the Force with the determination to "get on." I was the youngest constable to join and the youngest to gain the different ranks of promotion; and now in my retirement I have around me tokens - many most substantial and valuable - of the goodwill of communities magistrates, and officials with whom I have been associated. As I look upon these, the voluntary offerings of all sorts and conditions of men, I hope the reader will pardon my reflection that a life is worth living to meet with so much kindness and appreciation.

end